Lectures on the
Theory of Ethics (1812)

SUNY series in Contemporary Continental Philosophy

Dennis J. Schmidt, editor

Lectures on the
Theory of Ethics (1812)

J. G. Fichte

Translated, edited, and with an introduction by
Benjamin D. Crowe

Published by State University of New York Press, Albany

© 2015 State University of New York

All rights reserved

Printed in the United States of America

No part of this book may be used or reproduced in any manner whatsoever without written permission. No part of this book may be stored in a retrieval system or transmitted in any form or by any means including electronic, electrostatic, magnetic tape, mechanical, photocopying, recording, or otherwise without the prior permission in writing of the publisher.

For information, contact State University of New York Press, Albany, NY
www.sunypress.edu

Production, Eileen Nizer
Marketing, Michael Campochiaro

Library of Congress Cataloging-in-Publication Data

Fichte, Johann Gottlieb, 1762–1814.
 [Lectures. Selections. English]
 Lectures on the theory of ethics (1812) / J.G. Fichte ; translated, edited, and with an introduction by Benjamin D. Crowe.
     pages cm. — (SUNY series in contemporary continental philosophy)
 Includes bibliographical references and index.
 ISBN 978-1-4384-5869-4 (hc : alk. paper)—978-1-4384-5870-0 (pb : alk. paper)
 ISBN 978-1-4384-5871-7 (e-book)
 1. Ethics. I. Crowe, Benjamin D., 1976– translator, editor, writer of introduction. II. Title.

B2808 2015
170—dc23   2014049310

10 9 8 7 6 5 4 3 2 1

Contents

Editor's Introduction   vii

Lectures on the Theory of Ethics (1812)

Lecture 1	3
Lecture 2	9
Lecture 3	15
Lecture 4	21
Lecture 5	27
Lecture 6	33
Lecture 7	37
Lecture 8	43
Lecture 9	47
Lecture 10	53
Lecture 11	59
Lecture 12	65
Lecture 13	71
Lecture 14	77
Lecture 15	83
Lecture 16	89

Lecture 17	93
Lecture 18	99
Lecture 19	103
Lecture 20	107
Lecture 21	113
Lecture 22	119
Lecture 23	125
Lecture 24	131
Lecture 25	139
Lecture 26	145
Lecture 27	153
Lecture 28	159
Lecture 29	165
German–English Glossary	173
Index	177

Editor's Introduction

In recent decades the work of J. G. Fichte (1762–1814) has received sustained, serious, and sympathetic consideration. In the Anglophone world, this development has been fueled, in part, by new and authoritative translations of all of Fichte's important works from what is arguably the most influential period in his tumultuous intellectual career (1793–1800).[1] The situation is, however, somewhat different with respect to the period of Fichte's career that began with his move to Berlin and ended with his untimely death in 1814. Some of his later, more "popular" writings were translated in the nineteenth century, though these editions do not reflect the decades of serious textual work that have gone into the creation of the authoritative critical edition of Fichte's writings by an editorial team at the Bavarian Academy of Sciences. Fortunately, three of his works from the period after his departure from Jena in 1799 have recently been translated: (1) *The Closed Commercial State* (1801), an enigmatic treatise on political economy; (2) one series of lectures given in Berlin in 1804 on the *Wissenschaftslehre*; and (3) his epochal *Addresses to the German Nation* of 1808. Yet, it remains largely the case that Fichte's thought after 1800 is *terra incognita* to English speakers. The principal goal of the present translation is to begin to change this situation by providing an English edition of one of the most important pieces from Fichte's later years in Berlin, his lectures on the theory of ethics (*Sittenlehre*) delivered in the historically momentous year of 1812.

Why this text in particular? After all, there are other important works from this period, such as lectures on the core principles of the *Wissenschaftslehre* delivered in 1810, 1811, and 1812, that furnish a crucial window into this stage of Fichte's career and thus into a key phase of the development of German Idealism more generally. There are several reasons for the selection of the 1812 lectures on the theory of ethics. For one, as is discussed in more detail later, Fichte always regarded the development of practical philosophy (including ethics) as one of the key motivations of his entire philosophical endeavor. Moreover, his lectures on ethics address issues of serious philosophical import that are still alive in the present, including the nature of the will and of action, moral education, philosophy of history, and religion. Further, as his train of thought progresses through the lectures, Fichte takes time to engage with some of his contemporary rivals (e.g., Schelling). The lectures are, therefore, an important source for the way significant ideas were treated during this phase in the development of German Idealism.

Another reason is that, as mentioned previously, Fichte's *Addresses to the German Nation* are available in English, and scholars are beginning to reassess Fichte's place in the history of moral and political philosophy in light of this text. The 1812 lectures on ethics provide philosophical depth to many of the most prominent ideas in the *Addresses*, which, given the nature of the latter as a public speech, do not receive the same level of argumentative grounding as they do in the lecture course. To take one example, the lectures include a discussion of universal love or benevolence as the core of the moral point of view that forces one to carefully consider the nature of the messianic nationalism expressed in the *Addresses*.

In what follows, I introduce the lectures on the theory of ethics by contextualizing them, both historically and within Fichte's own system. I then provide an overview or outline of the content of the lectures themselves. To begin with, I describe the way in which the lectures can be profitably read against the background of the foundation of the new, reform-oriented University of Berlin. Fichte's vision of a reformed institution of higher learning influenced many of the key players in this momentous event, and the significance of the 1812 lectures emerges most clearly in light of his ongoing commitment to this vision. Next, I briefly review Fichte's other work in moral philosophy, as well as the overall place of ethics in his philosophical system. Having thus set forth the historical, institutional, and systematic background to the lectures, I conclude the main portion of my introductory comments with an outline of the lectures themselves. The outline is not meant to provide an exhaustive analysis of the content of the lectures. Instead, my hope is that this translation will spur others to undertake just such an analysis. What the outline is meant to accomplish is more modest, namely, the furnishing of a kind of orientation or road map that brings into focus some of the main ideas and argumentative transitions that belong to Fichte's train of thought.

The Context of the Lectures

For more than a century prior to Fichte's delivery of the lecture course on ethics in 1812, pressure had mounted within German academic and political circles for a radical reform of the nation's institutions of higher learning.² This reformist spirit had already resulted in the foundation of two new institutions at Halle (1694) and at Göttingen (1737). In fact, for a few years prior to the inauguration of the new university in Berlin in 1810, the former institution had been the place where many of these new ideas were implemented. The Treaty of Tilsit (1808), however, stripped Prussia of its premier university and so brought the experiment to an end. This geopolitical setback nevertheless cleared the path forward to the opening of a new university only two years later in Berlin.

Two aspects of this reformist spirit are particularly relevant to Fichte's teaching activities in Berlin after 1810, in general, and to the present lecture course, in particular. First, there was an effort to liberate the philosophical faculty within the academy from its subordinate position in relation to the "professional" faculties of law, medicine, and theology. Not only was philosophy to be granted the same level of prestige and support as the other faculties, it was to become the *central discipline*. One of the most influential arguments in this regard was provided by Kant in *The Conflict of the Faculties* (1798), a series of essays in which Kant made public some reflections rooted in his own struggles for academic freedom. Fichte's erstwhile friend and ally in the post-Kantian movement, F. W. J. Schelling, offered his own defense of the primacy of philosophy in lectures delivered in Würzburg in 1802 on "the method of academic study." Finally, Friedrich Schleiermacher's *Occasional Thoughts on Universities in the German Sense* (1808), published just prior to the actual establishment of the University of Berlin, likewise argued for the primacy of philosophy. As will become clear, Fichte shared this aspect of the reformers' program, and his lectures on ethics from 1812 closely follow both his own ideas regarding the centrality of philosophy within the academy as a whole and the carefully delineated architectonic of his own system, which was partially designed to reflect his view of the special function of philosophy.

The second element of this reformist spirit went beyond academic issues in a narrow sense, encompassing a vision of the moral vocation of university education within the whole of society. This feature of the reform agenda comes into stark relief when set against the background of the often riotous nature of student life in German universities, which was both lamented and satirized in the century prior to Fichte's teaching in Berlin. The tavern scene in Goethe's *Faust* is perhaps one of the most well-known depictions of the general moral climate of eighteenth-century universities. Starting in the 1780s, during Fichte's own time as a university student, he was steeped in literature that targeted the moral shortcomings of academic institutions, as well as in other works that championed new approaches to pedagogy more generally. This is apparent in an enigmatic fragment, most likely dating from 1788, called "Accidental Thoughts on a Sleepless Night," where, among other things, Fichte vigorously attacks the stultifying and corrupting influence of the contemporary educational system (II/1, 103–110). He cites a number of reformist works, such as Christian Gotthilf Salzmann's popular satirical novel, *Carl von Carlsberg, or On Human Misery* (published between 1784 and 1788). In an eerily prophetic section of the text, Salzmann relates a student riot occasioned by an effort to curtail the activities of fraternal organizations that closely parallels conflicts that Fichte himself faced regarding student discipline at Jena and at Berlin.

Further evidencing his own early commitment to the cause of educational reform, Fichte also enthusiastically refers in this fragment to the Swiss pedagogical reformer and theorist J. H. Pestalozzi's *Leonard and Gertrude: A Book for the People* (first edition, 1781). Over two decades later, Fichte still refers to Pestalozzi's ideas in a letter to his wife as "the true means of healing sick humanity" (III/6, 121). The 1808 *Addresses to the German Nation* contain lengthy discussions of Pestalozzi's later treatise, *How Gertrude Teaches Her Children* (1801). Fichte's commitment to the reform of the universities along both academic and moral lines endured throughout his entire life.

The University of Jena, where Fichte taught between 1794 and 1799, was a place where many of these reformist trends coalesced, and where, for a time, new ideas about education reform found a sympathetic hearing from those in power. Fichte was in the vanguard of the reformist movement in Jena, and from his privileged position as the leading exponent of post-Kantian idealism, he was able to influence many others. Following his relocation to Berlin, Fichte delivered several cycles of public lectures between 1804 and 1806 that drew individuals who wielded both cultural and political authority in the Prussian capital. Fichte continued to influence his contemporaries' thinking about the reform of German higher education. This period in Fichte's career reached its famous pinnacle in the 1808 *Addresses to the German Nation*, in which he argues that a new system of national education is the key to overcoming the moral and intellectual stagnation that he, like many others, blamed for the humiliation of Prussia by Napoleon's army.

In 1807 (the same year that Fichte praised Pestalozzi in the letter to his wife quoted earlier), the chief of the Prussian cabinet, K. F. Beyme, commissioned essays from some of the leading reformist academics of the realm, including Fichte (whom Beyme admired). What resulted was Fichte's

Deduced Plan of an Institute of Higher Learning to Be Established in Berlin (II/11, 65–170).[3] The statutes that were eventually adopted in founding the university owed more to Schleiermacher's 1808 essay referenced earlier. Nevertheless, the vision of the university that Fichte presents continued to guide his own activity as a teacher (and, for a brief period, university administrator) in ways that are still apparent in the 1812 lectures on ethics. Thus, it is useful to have in hand an overview of some of the main ideas presented in the *Deduced Plan*.

In §5, Fichte draws a distinction between accidental intellectual acquisitions and those that emerge from free conscious activity. The former are, for Fichte, not our own, as they derive from an obscure natural mechanism rather than from deliberate agency. As a corollary (made more explicit in the 1808 *Addresses to the German Nation*), Fichte maintains that only ideas of the latter sort can effectively ground a moral character. Such ideas are to be acquired through a dialogical process guided by a unifying idea (§§7–8). The idea that ultimately unifies this process ought to be the "root" of one's life as a whole, the core of the personality from which one approaches all activities. As such, this idea must be prior to, rather than derivative of, given realities (§10). Further, Fichte insists that this dialogical process must be animated by moral "respect [*Achtung*]" on the part of both teachers and students.

Following in Kant's footsteps, Fichte likewise attempts to subvert the traditionally subordinate status of the philosophical faculty within the hierarchy of disciplines in the university. Fichte argues that philosophy embraces and cultivates all of a person's intellectual powers, and that the conduct of genuine "science [*Wissenschaft*]" in any particular domain of inquiry requires that one be first of all a "philosophical artist" (§16). Among the consequences of this reversal of the traditional hierarchy is the fact that theology must become more philosophical, namely, that it cannot claim special authority on the basis of an inscrutable "mystery," and that its fundamental texts are no longer the only sources of moral insight (§22).

In February 1809, almost two years after Fichte and others submitted their reports to Beyme, Wilhelm von Humboldt assumed his own ministerial post. Humboldt knew Fichte and his ideas well, having interacted with him in Jena between 1794 and 1797 as a coeditor of Schiller's journal, *Die Horen*, and as an audience member at Fichte's "Morality for Scholars" lectures in 1794. The latter represent Fichte's first public presentation of many of the reformist ideals gestured at in "Accidental Thoughts on a Sleepless Night," including an insistence on the moral vocation of the university. Humboldt shared Fichte's lofty conception of this moral vocation, as well as the impulse to overturn the traditional disciplinary hierarchy in favor of philosophy. Later in 1809, Humboldt partly planted the seeds of the new university in Berlin by recruiting Fichte to deliver yet another series of public lectures in a disused palace that became the physical location of the institution upon its inauguration. Late in 1810, the University of Berlin opened its doors, with Fichte giving some of the very first lectures. In July 1811, Fichte began a brief tenure as the first elected rector of the university, and he used the occasion to deliver an inaugural address that further articulated and defended many of the ideas found in the 1807 *Deduced Plan*.[4] Thus, not long before the lectures in 1812 were delivered, Fichte clearly remained committed to these ideas.

History was not kind to Fichte and his 1812 lectures on ethics, nor indeed, at first, to the new University of Berlin. In June 1812, Napoleon's army crossed the Russian frontier. With the disintegration of his forces during the march back from Moscow, the so-called War of Liberation (or "War of the Sixth Coalition") began in earnest. Geopolitics thus overshadowed the first years of the new university and helped to distract most of the educated public from Fichte's first detailed treatment of ethics since his departure from Jena in 1799. Nonetheless, the foundation of a new university explicitly committed to many of the ideas Fichte himself cherished provides a context that helps to illuminate much of what he says in the 1812 lectures.

To begin with, the lectures contain a number of observations regarding the overall architectonic of Fichte's system. In the 1807 *Deduced Plan*, Fichte had argued that, in order to play its role as the unifying and guiding discipline of the entire academy, philosophy needed to be itself systematic. The professor of philosophy needs to have a clear sense of how his basic principles imply positions on every matter of philosophical import. In the 1812 lectures, this emphasis on a systematic architectonic shows up right away in Fichte's clarification of the distinction between *Wissenschaftslehre*, or the foundational layer of the system as a whole, and particular philosophical sciences such as the theory of ethics (*Sittenlehre*) (this point recurs, among other places, in Lecture 9).

The lectures on ethics also reflect Fichte's commitment to the primacy of philosophy within the constellation of academic disciplines. In Lecture 28, Fichte argues that the development of science must not be fettered by the requirement that scholars both profess and teach a creed (*Symbol*). He clearly defends the general necessity of a creed in articulating the deliverances of the moral consciousness in a way that can be agreed upon by the members of a community. Yet, he also insists that the creed cannot be regarded as immutable, and that the process of moral improvement within a community requires that the creed undergo continual refinement in light of the progress of moral and scientific insight. The responsibility for this refinement devolves upon a "scientific public" within the church community. In Lecture 29, Fichte explains the general division within this scientific public into *historical* and *philosophical* branches. In the *Deduced Plan* (§26), he had examined how the former is rooted in the more general disciplines of history (inclusive of the burgeoning discipline of the "history of the development of religious concepts and philology," the latter incorporating the study of biblical and "Oriental" languages with classics). Here, in the lectures on ethics, Fichte grants the historical branch of the "scientific public" a merely contingent significance, dependent on the role of sacred texts in a particular community. As in the *Deduced Plan*, Fichte rejects any effort to render a particular ancient text immune to critical analysis.[5] He also argues that none of the peoples of antiquity can claim a monopoly on moral truth, and that their textual legacies should all be mined for insights.

Fichte concludes the entire train of thought of the lectures by reminding his audience that philosophy encompasses the very same moral consciousness articulated (in a continually perfectible way) by a community's creed. Indeed, he argues that the rigor and clarity of philosophy is ultimately what is demanded by the underlying moral concept itself, and that the basic moral faith expressed in the creed ought to develop in the direction of philosophical insight. Philosophy thus becomes the highest judge of a historical faith (and, by extension, of its texts and creeds). In short, "the doctrine of philosophy regarding the supersensible is the pure faith toward which every ecclesiastical doctrine and creed must be elevated [. . .]."

As mentioned previously, Fichte was deeply committed to a central plank of the reformist agenda, namely, that the ultimate vocation of the university as an institution is a moral one. Thus, one is not at all surprised to see that his 1812 lectures on ethics articulate this guiding moral vision and its relationship to the scientific and educational enterprises of the university. For example, in Lecture 11, Fichte argues that pedagogy, or the science of the "reflective art [*besonnene Kunst*]" through which humanity is elevated to morality, falls out of the theory of ethics more generally. He distinguishes two senses of pedagogy: (1) a universal-historical sense that examines the way in which the human species as a whole progresses morally (borrowing from Lessing, Fichte calls this "the theory of education [*Erziehungslehre*] of the human species"); and (2) "pedagogy in the narrower sense," concerned with the education of children, the art of legislation, and religious education. The theory of ethics demands some account of how the "merely apparent I" comes to be a "true I," while it likewise furnishes the kind of clarity regarding the moral goal that is necessary for the formation of these subordinate disciplines in a rigorous, systematic manner.

As Fichte's train of thought unfolds in the lectures, he articulates the moral vision behind the reformed university. An important step is attained in Lecture 20, where Fichte makes explicit the connection between morality and science. The capacity to grasp ideas and goals that transcend one's private sphere (characterized by a mechanically functioning drive for self-preservation) is expressed and exemplified by science, an enterprise that is premised on the recognition of a common reason and a universal perspective toward which all should gradually converge. Fichte argues that this underlying recognition implies that knowledge must be shared and communicated, that is, it must be subjected to the public dialogical process that he had identified as the essence of activity in the university in the 1807 proposal. Science, like morality, involves a shared striving for a kind of rational identity (*Gleichheit*) beyond the idiosyncrasies of history and personality. This shared enterprise obliges those engaged in it to communicate their own points of view (*Ansichten*) and to confront and appropriate the challenges of others' points of view with the goal of cultivating a kind of rational harmony. Fichte goes on to argue that this harmony, brought about through reciprocal interaction, is a condition of the full realization of the moral concept, for only in this way can a perfected image of the ideal come to be. As he puts it in Lecture 22, the moral will strives for the "exhibition [*Darstellung*]" of the unity of reason through the "moralization of all, the upbuilding [*Erbauung*] of all."

In Lecture 21, Fichte contrasts this picture of a dialogical process inclusive of scientific debate with the approach of people who, while indeed inspired by rational ideas possessed of a kind of universality, seek to force this process of harmonization to its conclusion with "fire and sword." In Lecture 25, Fichte says that what morality demands is an attitude of "universal philanthropy" as the animating and controlling impulse behind the process of scientific-moral improvement. A direct consequence of this demand is that "no one can be moral for himself alone," that no one can be committed to the goal of morality without an active concern for the moral improvement of all. Thus, in the same lecture, Fichte qualifies the "separation" from the world recommended in the 1807 proposal (Fichte argues there that students should live in a kind of quasi-monastic community, insulated as far as possible from civic obligations, family life, etc.). This separation can only be temporary, a time in which one is dedicated to self-cultivation as a *means* for carrying out the philanthropic will. As he puts it in Lecture 25, "all scientific efforts must, without exception, be subordinated to the fundamental goal of earthly life, to the formation of the community for morality [. . .]." There are few more direct statements in Fichte's writings of the ultimate purpose of university studies.

The 1812 lectures on ethics can, therefore, be profitably read against the background of Fichte's lifelong interest in educational and university reform. Fichte is an important figure within a larger movement that had been gathering strength for some time. Napoleon's conquests, and the upheavals and dislocations they brought about, while regarded by many liberal-minded intellectuals as betrayals of the spirit of revolutionary France, nonetheless provided an opportunity for some of these same intellectuals' ideals to be tested in practice. The founding of the University of Berlin in 1810 can be seen as the culmination of the reformists' efforts, and Fichte was a central player in this cultural watershed. Fichte's 1812 lectures on ethics not only articulate the philosophical commitments underwriting his activities as an educator, they also document the way in which Fichte attempted to carry out these commitments in practice.

Fichte's Work on Ethics

In his own estimation, Fichte certainly regarded the theory of ethics (*Sittenlehre*) as the heart of the philosophical system that he endeavored to articulate and defend throughout his professional life.[6] While they may disagree about what precisely this entails, scholars tend to agree with Fichte that his particular brand of idealism is shaped at its deepest level by the "primacy of practical reason." In this introduction, I do not argue for my own views regarding what Fichte means by the primacy of practical reason, or about the substance of Fichte's theory of ethics. Here, I have the more modest aims of (1) indicating some of the facts regarding Fichte's treatment of ethics over his career and (2) substantiating the very general claim that ethics is the touchstone of Fichte's overall system.

During the periods of his career in which Fichte found himself steadily employed in an academic position, he devoted considerable energy to lecturing and publishing on ethics. In both of these periods, Fichte followed a similar pattern of lecture activity. Roughly, he divided his courses into (1) introductory lectures, (2) lectures on the fundamental principles of the *Wissenschaftslehre*, and (3) lectures on specific domains of philosophical inquiry. His teaching activity thus reflected the architectonic of his system, as well as the claim, made explicit in the 1807 *Deduced Plan*, that such an architectonic is a necessary condition for successful philosophical education. Based on his vision of the nature of his philosophical system, Fichte was convinced that students (or even the general public) could only fully appreciate its central claims if they had been educated in the proper way. This entailed (1) coming to understand the social role of the intellectual in general and (2) achieving the proper standpoint from which to engage the intricacies of transcendental philosophy. Once this had been accomplished, Fichte could then present the most basic principles of his *Wissenschaftslehre*, in which he endeavored to articulate the transcendental conditions of human experience. The basic concepts and explanatory structures revealed by the *Wissenschaftslehre* could then be used to construct an idealist account of the traditional domains of philosophical investigation, which Fichte typically divided into nature, society (including law and politics), morality, and religion.[7]

While in Jena, Fichte lectured on the theory of ethics during the summer term of 1796, the winter term of 1796/97, and again during the winter term of 1797/98. During the winter term of 1798/99, which proved to see the ignominious conclusion of his professorship in Jena, Fichte gave a combined lecture on natural right and ethics. During this period, Fichte published his first and only systematic treatise devoted entirely to the subject. *The System of Ethics according to the Principles of the Wissenschaftslehre* first appeared in printed fascicles for the use of students attending his 1797/98 course. It was published as a book in its own right in June 1798. As is true of the lectures translated here, it would be a mistake to regard the *System of Ethics* of 1798 as a work narrowly focused on moral theory as it is usually understood and pursued by philosophers today. Instead, Fichte's discussion ranges much more broadly, ultimately encompassing some of his clearest discussions of his basic philosophical orientation as well as key aspects of the foundational portion of his system.

Other than a brief academic appointment (in Erlangen in 1805), Fichte did not resume formal teaching in an institution of higher learning until 1810, when he took up his chair at the University of Berlin. During this final phase of his career, Fichte's teaching activity followed a pattern largely similar to the one he had first pursued in Jena, namely, introductory lectures, *Wissenschaftslehre* proper, specific philosophical disciplines. He did, however, add two new components. The first, called "The Facts of Consciousness" (held four times, in the winter term 1810/11, summer term 1811, winter term 1811/12, and winter term 1812/13) explicitly aimed to provide his students with a thorough initiation into philosophy. The second new element consisted in lectures on transcendental logic (held twice, in summer term 1812 and winter term 1812/13), which had both an introductory and a more systematic purpose.[8] Unlike in Jena, Fichte only offered one course on ethics, in the summer term of 1812. The reason for this lies in historical exigencies. On June 23, shortly before Fichte began the lectures, Napoleon's army crossed the Russian frontier. Early in 1813, Fichte's teaching was curtailed by the start of the so-called War of the Sixth Coalition, which continued until the following spring, concluding after Fichte had died. No doubt, Fichte would have followed the pattern begun in Jena and delivered many more lectures on ethics had these events, which led directly to his death, not intervened.

As in the case of the *System of Ethics* of 1798, the 1812 lectures on the theory of ethics range across a great many topics. These include the nature of idealism (in contrast to other systems, such as Schelling's *Naturphilosophie*), the structure of the will and of action, practical reasoning, moral education, the relation between morality and religion, the philosophical analysis of revelation (a topic Fichte had been contemplating since even before arriving in Jena), and even, albeit inexplicitly and somewhat *sotto voce*, Napoleon's crossing of the Russian frontier in June 1812.

The Position of Ethics in Fichte's Thought

As mentioned previously, there is no question that ethics stands at the very center of Fichte's philosophical project. Fichte maintains that his idealism is the only philosophical position that can fully justify and explain morality. By the same token, grasping the significance of Fichte's idealism ultimately requires coming to terms with his account of morality. This is something that Fichte makes abundantly clear, both in the earlier and later parts of his career.

Just prior to embarking upon his tumultuous professorship in Jena, Fichte writes to a friend, disclosing that he sees his primary contribution to philosophy in the wake of Kant to lie in his ability to render a consistent account of "freedom" and of the "practical imperative" (III/2, 28). Elsewhere, he confides that the ultimate outcome of his new idealism is meant to be "a new, nobler, more worthy species" (III/2, 50–51). In a draft letter from the spring of 1795, Fichte likewise points to ethics as the domain in which his primary contribution lies:

> My system is the first *system of freedom*. Just as [France] has shattered the chains of human beings, so too my theory frees the

person from the fetters of the thing-in-itself and its influence, which more or less constrained him in all previous systems; and through the exalted attitude [*Stimmung*] that it communicates, it gives the person power to also free himself in practice. (III/2, 300)

More famously, in a 1797 essay called *An Attempt at a New Presentation of the Wissenschaftslehre*, Fichte has this to say about the relationship between his idealism and ethics:

The kind of philosophy one chooses thus depends upon the kind of person one is. For a philosophical system is not a lifeless household item one can put aside or pick up as one wishes; instead, it is animated by the very soul of the person who adopts it. Someone whose character is naturally slack or who has been enervated and twisted by spiritual servitude, scholarly self-indulgence, and vanity will never be able to raise himself to the level of idealism (I/4, 195/IW, 20).

People have been debating just what it is that Fichte is claiming in this passage virtually since the moment it was printed. While the scholarly debate is outside the scope of this introduction, it is safe to presume that at least part of what Fichte is saying here is that there is an intimate connection between a certain moral character and idealism as a philosophical outlook, and that the latter in some sense expresses or does justice to the former in a way other philosophical positions do not.

Comments to this effect are by no means isolated to writings from the Jena period. In his lectures on the *Wissenschaftslehre* from 1810, Fichte maintains that the "real life of the *ethical* person" is the true touchstone of philosophy, a claim he attributes also to Kant (StA I, 90). "In the dominant schools [of philosophy] that were maintained [prior to Kant] there was no longer any talk of genuine morality [*Sittlichkeit*], of a purpose beyond all nature and time, or of elevation above these" (StA I, 90). While an "obscure intimation" of morality and "even religiosity" are possible aside from the *Wissenschaftslehre*, the latter brings with it the "clarity of the concept" (StA I, 94). In the lectures on the *Wissenschaftslehre* from 1812, Fichte asserts the superiority of idealism in similar terms. It alone can account adequately for our "moral nature," for the fact that we "are and *ought to be* free," that reason is "practical and moral" (II/13, 163). This account is nothing less than "[t]he high point and the purest expression of the idealism of the *Wissenschaftslehre* for which I wanted to prepare the way [. . .]. The scales of dogmatism and *Naturphilosophie* will fall from the eyes of whoever understands this" (II/13, 163). If we take these and other statements made by Fichte throughout his career seriously, then it must be concluded that a proper understanding of his distinctive approach to philosophy can only be achieved by carefully attending to his theory of ethics.

Outline of the Lectures

The entire course of lectures was offered by Fichte in twenty-nine installments, beginning on June 29, 1812, and concluding on August 13. Fichte had concluded his lectures on the theory of right (*Rechtslehre*) on June 17. Both of these lecture series had been announced in the university's catalog for the summer term as "philosophical sciences." Overlapping with the theory of ethics, Fichte delivered the first of two lecture courses on transcendental logic (between April 20 and August 14). A heavily edited text of the lectures on ethics, combining both Fichte's own manuscript and material from a student transcript, was published by Fichte's son I. H. Fichte in 1835 and reissued in 1912. There are three extant original versions of the lecture material apart from this earlier edition: (1) Fichte's own manuscript, (2) a transcript by Jakob Ludwig Cauer, and (3) a transcript by an unknown hand, called the "Halle transcript" due to the fact that it is preserved in the city archives of the old university town of Halle.

Fichte begins the lecture with a brief discussion of the relationship between the theory of ethics, as a particular "philosophical science," and the foundational portion of the *Wissenschaftslehre*. The theory of ethics is the analysis of the claim that "the concept is the ground of the world," or rather, it is the derivation of the conditions for the possibility of the concept being the ground of the world. Fichte links this part of his discussion with the theory of concepts developed contemporaneously in his lectures on transcendental logic. The concept that is supposed to ground the world cannot, in this instance, be copied from the world but must be "absolute" or "pure." This starting point parallels that of the 1798 *System of Ethics*, where Fichte explicates the conditions upon which reason can be practical. In this way, despite the distinctively Fichtean idiom, the 1812 lectures also reflect Fichte's Kantian heritage.

The first condition that Fichte derives is that the pure concept cannot become the ground of the world unless we assume that there is *life*, or self-determining activity. For the concept to become the ground of the world there must be something that brings this state of affairs about. But, it turns out that sheer life in the biological sense is not sufficient; for the *concept* to become the ground of the world, we need to add consciousness; the life that is required is one that determines itself according to a "paradigm" (*Vorbild*) or a representation of some state of the world. As Fichte puts it, we need life with an "eye." Fichte now explains that self-determination in accordance with a concept is what he means by the *will*. A will that is capable of bringing about a state of affairs in accord with an "absolute" or "pure" concept, however, must be something that is not solely or entirely determined by the natural drive.

With these conditions in place, Fichte goes on to argue that ethics becomes "real" only when this capacity for self-determination according to a pure concept is seen as the "absolute determination of the I." That is, one comes to see that any action that one pursues must ultimately be consistent with this essential feature of I-hood. This purely *intelligible* concept is precisely the pure concept in accordance with which some state of affairs in the world is to be brought forth. According to Fichte, this condition is what Kant tries to express by means of the categorical imperative. An agent acts according to a "paradigm" or image of some state of the world, and for this action to be properly moral, this state of the world has to be consistent with the "absolute determination of the I" just described.

Fichte next argues that moral action is only possible on the condition that this supersensible or intelligible concept of the essence of the I "appears," that is, is somehow present for an agent in her consciousness. According to Fichte, this point is expressed theologically by the doctrine of the Incarnation. Yet, it is not sufficient that the concept in question merely be grasped or recognized; rather it must appear with obligatory force, as an "ought." Moral action rests upon an agent's cognition of this absolute norm *as a norm*. At this point, Fichte finds himself required to differentiate two standpoints on the entire topic: (1) that of the *theory of being* and (2) that of the *theory of appearance*. The former standpoint, according to which the I and its freedom are deduced from the absolute concept, leaves no room for obligatory force, since the very being of freedom is a necessary product of the concept. The latter standpoint, on the other hand, is the one from which it makes sense to inquire about moral normativity and its bearing on the wills of finite agents.[9] This theory of appearance, or moral phenomenology, as Fichte calls it, becomes the main focus of the discussion throughout the remainder of the lectures. He sets out the formal structure of this theory in Lecture 13, distinguishing between moral appearance (which always involves the I's reflective awareness of itself as the expression of the concept) and immoral appearance. Fichte then goes on to discuss how moral appearance involves the establishment of an enduring character or disposition that, as it were, anticipates one's future acts of willing to do one's duty.

One of Fichte's central claims is that the cognition of the pure concept as normative requires moral formation. He first explains that the moral formation of the individual is something that presupposes the formation of the human species as a whole. The latter, Fichte maintains, can be thought of as something that falls ultimately under the power of God. The end result of the process of moral formation for any particular individual is that one should come to see oneself as the "appearance" of the pure concept, or as the "image of God." God's education of the human species, given the goal at which it aims, must obviously be consistent with self-determination. More specifically, the content of the educative process is supposed to be the motive of one's action, but this content must be consistent with the nature of agency as described earlier. This means that mechanical causal influence is ruled out as a means for moral formation.

Fichte next turns to a consideration of the stages of this process of moral formation, a process that he retraces elsewhere in his lectures on the "facts of consciousness." The first stage is simply the awareness of oneself as an agent capable of influencing the states of affairs of the empirical world (corresponding to the bare biological concept of life described previously). Next, one must come to think of oneself as more than a merely natural being, since only in this way can a person begin to comprehend the idea of freedom. According to Fichte, this requires the concept of a "community of I's" sharing a common rationality and thus capable of being bound by principles that are genuinely universal.[10] At this point, we have reached the first glimmering of the properly moral standpoint. This is expressed by the idea that each individual should be brought to harmonize with others in a way that gradually abstracts away from their particularities as natural beings, leading to a state more closely approximating the common rationality referred to previously. More concretely, this means that any state of affairs of the empirical world must be seen as subservient to this harmonization. Fichte points out how there are many goals or ends—economic, political, aesthetic, or religious—that are not reducible to merely natural desires and that in many cases produce profound and lasting changes in the empirical world. Here he refers to the Prophet Muhammad's zeal for monotheism. He also alludes in a more subtle way to Napoleon's recent invasion of the Russian Empire, an event of undoubted historical significance and yet, on Fichte's view, of dubious moral value. Indeed, Fichte insists that the fact that great deeds result from these motives is beside the point from a moral point of view.

The goal of the harmonization of humanity as a whole in accord with our shared rationality must be present to an individual in the first instance in an "image" or "representational concept." That is, a person must have some particular idea of a state of affairs that accords with duty, which can be thought of as a kind of limitation or determination of the universal goal described in the preceding paragraph. Fichte argues that, for most people, this is entirely sufficient, though it is not the highest form of the moral point of view. For the latter, one must explicitly take as the object of one's will the morality of every person, that is, each person's complete identification with his or her being the "image of God." Or, as he puts it further on, one's explicit aim ought to be "the moralizing of all, the upbuilding [*Erbauung*] of all into a single ethical community." One's action should be for the sake of the freedom of all. For Fichte, this is what it means to say that *love* is the highest form of morality. Given the content of this aim, it is evident that it cannot be achieved through violence or coercion, since genuine morality must be consistent with free self-determination. This claim is particularly interesting in light of the appropriation of Fichte's earlier *Addresses to the German Nation* in the cause of militaristic nationalism in the later nineteenth and twentieth centuries.

Internally, that is, to the moral agent, the moral character is manifest first of all as self-denial, or the relinquishing of mere survival as one's highest end. Second, it is expressed by "universal philanthropy"; that is, humanity, not one's contingent desires as a natural being, forms one's highest object. Finally, this universal philanthropy is incompatible with simply avoiding interference in other people's affairs. It is an active concern with the morality of all, one that requires full engagement in a community. This is not to say, of course, that there is no room for self-cultivation (e.g., scientific study) in a more private manner, though this must always be subordinated to the end of morality. Fichte goes on to specify honesty or truthfulness, as well as simplicity, as defining features of the truly moral character.

In the final portion of the lectures, Fichte argues that a further essential condition for the realization of morality is a *church*. The church first of all preserves the collective wisdom of humanity, for history as a totality embodies a cultivated humanity. Second, the church must be unified by a creed, by a determinate vision of the moral community or of the vocation of humanity. The creed itself rests ultimately on revelation, which Fichte conceives of as the process whereby an inspired individual becomes conscious of this vision and then communicates it to other people in such a way that their "moral sense" concurs with it. Any particular creed may come to deviate from the original revelation; Fichte maintains that we can see that this has happened when we compare the teachings of Jesus in John's Gospel with some of the later dogmas of the church. The possibility of this kind of deviation, however, does not entail that the particular insights or interpretations of individuals could somehow replace the creed. Rather, the duty of the educated members of the church is to progressively perfect the creed in the light of the initial revelation.

In line with what he had argued previously about the inconsistency between coercion and the end of morality, Fichte argues that consent to the creed can only rest on the moral sense or on an "inner demonstration," never on *force majeure* or some other external authority. It may turn out that a church founded on authority does promote the moral progress of humanity, but Fichte regards this as a matter of luck, whereas a church united by a creed that people accept on the basis of conscience does not have the same sort of merely contingent relation to this progress. Historical knowledge (e.g., of the authorship of texts) plays no role in producing conviction here, though it might be of use in the process of revising the creed to accord with the original inspiration. Philosophy, on the other hand, since it shares the "same content" with the creed, is much more central to this revision process. Interestingly, Fichte argues that "moral faith" is the presupposition for philosophy, that the church is the "fold" from which the philosopher springs. Moral faith is the initial mode in which the content of morality is given; only when it is given can it be philosophically clarified.

Note on Translation

As mentioned earlier, there are three extant original texts of Fichte's 1812 lectures on ethics. The authoritative critical edition of Fichte's works, produced by an editorial team with the Bavarian Academy of the Sciences, contains two of these in complete form: (1) series II, volume 13, contains Fichte's own manuscript; and (2) series IV, volume 6, contains the Halle transcript. Cauer's transcript is not reproduced in its entirety but is instead occasionally included in footnotes to both of these texts. The state of this transcript is reflected in the present translation by the absence of pagination when it is cited. More recently, a new critical edition of Fichte's manuscript has appeared in StA, under the general editorship of Hans Georg von Manz, which makes several (unspecified) corrections to the GA version. The present translation is a complete, continuous rendering of Fichte's manuscript according to the newer StA version. Supplemental materials from both transcripts are included in footnotes. I have provided pagination for both the GA and StA versions for the benefit of those who read German and are interested in comparing the translation with both versions.

I have organized the translation into chapters corresponding to the date on which the lectures were originally delivered by Fichte. I have endeavored to produce a text that is both accurate and readable. This has turned out to be no small task, as Fichte's manuscript often reads more like a series of shorthand notes to himself than a polished text. The 1812 lectures on the theory of ethics is a challenging text; indeed, it represents some of the most difficult prose Fichte ever produced.

In addition to the pagination, other notations in the text are as follows: {. . .}, supplemental interpolations provided by the editors of the GA volumes; [. . .], supplemental interpolations provided by me, including reproductions of the original German text; and |, page breaks in the originals of Fichte's manuscript.[11]

Selected English and German Bibliography

There is virtually no English-language scholarly literature that directly deals with the 1812 lectures on the theory of ethics. There are several works that engage moral and political philosophy and Fichte's later philosophy more generally, which I have listed in this section. Readers who know German might also find it useful to have some additional orientation toward the text through a bibliography of recent (i.e., from the last two decades) scholarship.

Selected Translations of Fichte's Writings into English

Adler, Anthony C., trans. *The Closed Commercial State*. Albany: State U of New York P, 2012.

Breazeale, Daniel, and Günter Zöller, eds. *The System of Ethics in accordance with the Principles of the Wissenschaftslehre*. Cambridge: Cambridge UP, 2005. (This is a translation of the 1798 *System der Sittenlehre*.)

Estes, Yolanda, and Curtis Bowman, eds. *J. G. Fichte and the Atheism Dispute (1798–1800)*. Burlington: Ashgate, 2010. (Contains important texts dealing with the development of Fichte's philosophy of religion.)

Moore, Gregory, trans. *Addresses to the German Nation*. Cambridge: Cambridge UP, 2008.

Preuss, Peter, trans. *The Vocation of Man*. Indianapolis: Hackett, 1987.
Smith, William, ed., *The Popular Works of Johann Gottlieb Fichte*. Introduction by Daniel Breazeale. Bristol: Thoemmes Press, 1999. (This translation includes three works from 1806: *Der Grundzüge des gegenwärtigen Zeitalters, Über das Wesen des Gelehrten, und seine Erscheinungen im Gebiete der Freiheit,* and *Anweisung zum seeligen Leben, oder auch die Religionslehre*. The translation originally appeared between 1848 and 1889.)
Wright, Walter E., trans. "The Science of Knowledge in its General Outline." *Idealistic Studies* 6 (1976): 106–117. (This is a translation of the 1810 *Die Wissenschaftslehre, in ihrem allgemeinen Umrisse dargestellt*.)
Wright, Walter E., trans. *The Science of Knowing: Fichte's 1804 Lectures on the Wissenschaftslehre*. Albany: State U of New York P, 2005.

Monographs

Asmuth, Christoph. *Das Begreifen des Unbegreiflichen: Philosophie und Religion bei Johann Gottlieb Fichte*. Stuttgart-Bad Cannstatt: Frommann-Holzboog, 1998.
Brachtendorf, Johannes. *Fichtes Lehre vom Sein: Eine kritische Darstellung der Wissenschaftslehren von 1794, 1798/99, und 1812*. Paderborn: Ferdinand Schonigh, 1995.
Breazeale, Daniel. *Thinking through the Wissenschaftslehre: Themes from Fichte's Early Philosophy*. Cambridge: Cambridge UP, 2013.
James, David. *Fichte's Social and Political Philosophy: Property and Virtue*. Cambridge: Cambridge UP, 2011.
Janke, Wolfgang. *Die dreifache Vollendung des deutschen Idealismus: Schelling, Hegel, und Fichtes ungeschriebene Lehre*. Amsterdam: Rodopi, 2008.
Janke, Wolfgang. *Vom Bilde des Absoluten: Grundzüge der Phänomenologie Fichtes*. Berlin and New York: De Gruyter, 1993.
Lauth, Reinhard. *Vernünftige Durchdringung der Wirklichkeit: Fichte und sein Umkreis*. Neuried bei München: ars una Verlagsgesellschaft, 1994.
Oesterreich, Peter L., and Hartmut Traub. *Der ganze Fichte: Die populäre, wissenschaftliche und metaphilosophische Erschließung der Welt*. Stuttgart: Kohlhammer, 2006.
Schmid, Dirk. *Religion und Christentum in Fichtes Spätphilosophie 1810–1813*. Berlin and New York: De Gruyter, 1995.
Siep, Ludwig. *Praktische Philosophie im deutschen Idealismus*. Frankfurt: Suhrkamp, 1992.

Edited Volumes

Fuchs, Erich, Marco Ivaldo, and Giovanni Moretto, ed. *Der transzendentalphilosophische Zugang zur Wirklichkeit: Beiträge aus der aktuellen Fichte-Forschung*. Stuttgart-Bad Cannstatt: Frommann-Holzboog, 2001.
Rockmore, Tom, and Daniel Breazeale, ed. *After Jena: New Essays on Fichte's Later Philosophy*. Evanston: Northwestern UP, 2008.

Von Manz, Hans Georg, and Günter Zöller, ed. *Fichtes praktische Philosophie: Eine systematische Einführung.* Hildesheim: Olms, 2006.

Special Journal Volumes

Fichte-Studien. Vol. 8. "Religionsphilosophie." Ed. Klaus Hammacher, Richard Schottky, and Wolfgang H. Schrader. Amsterdam: Rodopi, 1995.

Fichte-Studien, Vol. 15. "Transcendentale Logik." Ed. Klaus Hammacher and Richard Schottky. Amsterdam: Rodopi, 1999.

Fichte-Studien, Vol. 20. "Zur Wissenschaftslehre. Beiträge zum vierten Kongress der Internationalen Johann-Gottlieb-Fichte-Gesellschaft in Berlin vom 03.–08. Oktober 2000." Ed. Helmut Girndt. Amsterdam: Rodopi, 2003.

Fichte-Studien, Vol. 23. "Praktische und angewandte Philosophie I: Beiträge zum vierten Kongress der Internationalen Johann-Gottlieb-Fichte-Gesellschaft in Berlin vom 03.–08. Oktober 2000." Ed. Helmut Girndt and Helmut Traub. Amsterdam: Rodopi, 2003.

Fichte-Studien, Vol. 24. "Praktische und angewandte Philosophie II: Beiträge zum vierten Kongress der Internationalen Johann-Gottlieb-Fichte-Gesellschaft in Berlin vom 03.–08. Oktober 2000." Ed. Helmut Girndt and Hartmut Traub. Amsterdam: Rodopi, 2003.

Fichte-Studien, Vol. 27. "Die Sittenlehre J. G. Fichtes 1798–1812." Ed. Christoph Asmuth and Wilhelm Metz. Amsterdam: Rodopi 2006.

Fichte-Studien, Vol. 28. "Fichtes letzte Darstellungen der Wissenschaftslehre. Beiträge zum Fünften Internationalen Fichte-Kongreß 'Johann Gottlieb Fichte: Das Spätwerk (1810–1814) und das Lebenswerk' in München vom 14. bis 21. Oktober 2003. Teil I." Ed. Günter Zöller and Hans Georg von Manz. Amsterdam: Rodopi, 2006.

Fichte-Studien, Vol. 29. "Praktische Philosophie in Fichtes Spätwerk: Beiträge zum Fünften Internationalen Fichte-Kongreß 'Johann Gottlieb Fichte. Das Spätwerk (1810–1814) und das Lebenswerk' in München vom 14. bis 21 Oktober 2003. Teil II." Ed. Günter Zöller and Hans Georg von Manz. Amsterdam: Rodopi, 2006.

Journal Articles and Book Chapters

Abizadeh, Arash. "Was Fichte an Ethnic Nationalist? On Cultural Nationalism and Its Double." *History of Political Thought* 26 (2005): 334–359.

Düsing, Edith. "Sittliches Streben und religiöse Vereinigung: Untersuchungen zu Fichtes später Religionsphilosophie." In *Religionsphilosophie und spekulative Theologie: Der Streit um die Göttlichen Dinge (1799–1812)*, ed. Walter Jaeschke. Hamburg: Felix Meiner, 1994. 98–128.

Edmondson, Nelson. "The Fichte Society: A Chapter in Germany's Conservative Revolution." *Journal of Modern History* 38 (1966): 161–180.

Husserl, Edmund. "Fichte's Ideal of Humanity [Three Lectures]," trans. James G. Hart. *Husserl Studies* 12 (1995): 111–133.

Ivaldo, Marco. "Ethik der Inkarnation in J. G. Fichtes Vorlesungen über die Sittenlehre 1812." In *Rozum Jest Wolny, Wolnosc-Rozumna, Festschrift zum 60: Geburtstag von Marek J. Siemek*, ed. Robert Marszalek and Ewa Novak-Juchacz. Warsaw: Polskiej Akademii Nauk, 2002. 101–116.

Ivaldo, Marco. "Transzendentale Lebenslehre: Zur Königsberger Wissenschaftslehre 1807." *Perspektiven der Philosophie* 22 (1996): 167–188.

Janke, Wolfgang. "'Das Wissen ist an sich die absolute Existenz.' Der oberste Grundsatz in Fichtes 4. Vortrag der Wissenschaftslehre, Erlangen im Sommer 1805." *Perspektiven der Philosophie* 22 (1996): 189–230.

Janke, Wolfgang. "Menschenliebe. Aufriß einer Theorie ethisch-religiöser Grundaffekte im Anschluß an Fichtes Religionslehre von 1806." In *Person und Sinnerfahrung: Philosophische Grundlagen und interdisziplinäre Perspektiven, Festschrift für Georg Scherer zum 65. Geburtstag*, ed. Carl Friedrich Gethmann and Peter L. Oesterreich. Darmstadt: Wissenschaftliche Buchgesellschaft, 1993. 91–100.

Moggach, Douglas. "Fichte's Engagement with Machiavelli." *History of Political Thought* 14 (1993): 573–589.

Schottky, Richard. "Fichtes Nation-Begriff 1806 bis 1813—In der Spannung und Entwicklung." In *Gesellschaft, Staat, Nation*, ed. Rudolf Burger, Hans-Dieter Klein, Wolfgang R. Schrader. Wien: Verlag der österreicheschen Akademie der Wissenschaften, 1996. 159–184

Sluga, Hans. "Fichte, Nietzsche, and the Nazis." In *Heidegger's Crisis*. Cambridge: Harvard UP, 1993. 29–52.

Zöller, Günter. "Das Absolute und seine Erscheinung: Die Schelling-Rezeption des späten Fichte." In *Recht–Moral–Selbst: Gedenkschrift für Wolfgang H. Schrader*, ed. Marion Heinz und Klaus Hammacher. Hildesheim: Olms, 2004. 311–328.

Notes

1. References to Fichte's works are given parenthetically in the text according to the following abbreviations:

Original language editions:

GA J.-G. Fichte. *Gesamtausgabe der Bayerischen Akademie der Wissenschaften*. Ed. Reinhard Lauth, Hans Jacobs, Hans Gliwitzky, and Erich Fuchs, 42 vols. Stuttgart-Bad Canstatt: Frommann-Holzboog, 1962–2012.

StA Johann Gottlieb Fichte. *Die späten wissenschaftlichen Vorlesungen*. Ed. Hans Georg von Manz et al., 3 vols. Stuttgart-Bad Canstatt: Frommann-Holzboog, 2000–.

English translations:
IW Daniel Breazeale, trans. *Introductions to the Wissenschaftslehre and Other Writings.* Indianapolis: Hackett, 1994.

2. My discussion in this section relies on a number of excellent scholarly examinations of the history of university reform in Germany and of the foundation of the University of Berlin in particular. An English-language discussion that is particularly useful for readers generally interested in this topic is Theodore Ziolkowski, *German Romanticism and Its Institutions* (Princeton: Princeton UP, 1990). Another excellent account that incorporates Fichte within the larger discussions of the period is Richard Crouter, *Friedrich Schleiermacher: Between Enlightenment and Romanticism* (Cambridge: Cambridge UP, 2005), ch. 6. Regarding the University of Berlin in particular, the classic studies in German are Rudolf Köpke, *Die Gründung der königlichen Friedrich-Wilhelms-Universität zu Berlin* (Berlin: Schade, 1860) and Max Lenz, *Geschichte der Königlichen Friedrich-Wilhelms-Universität zu Berlin*, 2 vols. (Halle: Verlag der Buchhandlung des Waisenhauses, 1910). A helpful English-language study of the origins of the new institution in Berlin is Charles E. McClelland, *State, Society, and University in Germany 1700–1914* (Cambridge: Cambridge UP, 1980).

3. Some of Fichte's other, lesser-known, writings on pedagogy from his time in Berlin include "Aphorisms on Education" (1804; II/7, 7–22) and notes on the organization of the University of Erlangen (1805; II/9, 327–380).

4. See I/10, 347–377.

5. This comports with Fichte's position, spelled out in Lecture 16, that moral reform must proceed in accord with the "law of freedom," that is, it must employ concepts and reasons in order to bring about shifts in moral awareness. The use of merely "mechanical means" (e.g., physical compulsion or inexplicable natural occurrences) is thus ruled out. In the *Deduced Plan*, Fichte had likewise argued that theology can only take up a place within the reformed university if it abjures mystery in favor of rational analysis.

6. Interestingly, it has recently been shown that Fichte's ethics was regarded for many decades as the epitome of post-Kantian moral philosophy, even, to some extent, surpassing Kant's own works as sources in later discussions. See Michelle Kosch, "Fichtean Kantianism in Nineteenth-Century Ethics," *Journal of the History of Philosophy* 53 (1) (2015): 111–132.

7. For an excellent overview of the structure and goals of Fichte's philosophical system, see Daniel Breazeale, "The Spirit of the *Wissenschaftslehre*," in *The Reception of Kant's Critical Philosophy: Fichte, Schelling, and Hegel*, ed. Sally Sedgwick (Cambridge: Cambridge UP, 2000), 171–198.

8. During his time at Jena, Fichte held "propaedeutic" lectures for his students more or less every semester between the winter term of 1794/95 and the winter term of 1798/99. These courses were entitled Logic and Metaphysics. Fichte used the *Philosophische Aphorismen* of the Enlightenment *Populärphilosoph* Ernst Platner as a kind of textbook. Despite the title, however, these lectures do

not provide the sort of sustained discussion of transcendental logic that Fichte presented later in Berlin. Thus, it is safe to treat the latter as a new component of his teaching activity.

9. There is a close parallel here between Fichte's distinction between these two standpoints and Kant's conception of noumenal affection or causation. The latter had inspired debate ever since C. C. E. Schmid proposed "intelligible fatalism" as a solution to lingering problems in the Kantian theory. For recent discussions of these issues, see Allen Wood, "Kant's Compatibilism," in *Kant's Critique of Pure Reason: Critical Essays*, ed. Patricia Kitcher (London: Rowman & Littlefield, 1998), 239–263; Michelle Kosch, *Freedom and Reason in Kant, Schelling, and Kierkegaard* (Oxford: Clarendon Press, 2006); and Christopher Insole, *Kant and the Creation of Freedom* (Oxford: Oxford UP, 2013).

10. In fact, Fichte presents a new deduction of intersubjectivity or of the necessity for a plurality of subjects in these lectures, beginning with Lecture 17 and continuing thence, through a number of dense and difficult paragraphs, until Lecture 20.

11. I would like to thank Hans Georg von Manz (Ludwig-Maximilians Universität, Munich) and Erich H. Fuchs (Bayerische Akademie der Wissenschaften, Fichte-Kommission) for graciously providing me with advice on the texts and on translation matters, and for making available to me the Cauer transcript, edited by Ives Radrizzani (Ludwig-Maximilians Universität, Munich). I am grateful to the Philosophy Department at the University of Utah for granting me leave during the academic year 2013-14 to complete the work for this translation, as well as to the Philosophy Department at Temple University for affording me a visiting position and research resources during that time. I owe a particular debt to Kristin Gjesdal (Temple University) for her warm hospitality and many helpful conversations. I am likewise grateful to Andew Kenyon, Laurie Searl, and Eileen Nizer at SUNY Press for their hard work in preparing this volume for publication and for guiding me through the entire process, and to Leonard Rosenbaum for preparing the index.

Lectures on the
Theory of Ethics (1812)

Lecture 1

(June 29, 1812)

StA 269
GA II/13,
307

Morality.
This lecture on the theory of ethics [*Sittenlehre*] must be understood as [treating] a distinct, individual topic.

[The theory of ethics] is a particular *philosophical* science, not philosophy or the *Wissenschaftslehre* itself. It therefore assumes a fact (that such and such is the case) without further demonstration; the demonstration, the derivation from a whole, belongs to the *Wissenschaftslehre*.[1, 2] This constitutes the distinctiveness [of this science]. This [fact] is a *presupposition*. {The theory of ethics educes [*entwickelt*]} what *follows* from the presupposition; to that extent, then, it certainly is deductive. [It is] a philosophical theory of knowing, for {it is related to} a fact of *consciousness*. This should not be ignored. (In this manner, [the science] acquires clarity [*Deutlichkeit*]; it is a simple [*bloße*] analysis [carried out] with care and in writing).

The fact [that belongs] to the *theory of ethics* [is stated in the following way]: *let the concept be the ground of the world,* with the *absolute consciousness, that* it is [the ground

---

1. CAUER: Here, as in every particular philosophical science, a fact that is presupposed in a problematic way is taken as a basis.
2. HALLE: [. . .] a *particular* science that must be grounded on *a fact*, not the *Wissenschaftslehre* itself but rather a part of it. [This science] presupposes a fact: such and such exists. The essence of science is *to derive* [*herzuleiten*] [something] from such a presupposition, to *analyze* it completely. [This science] presupposes a fact that *is* not further demonstrated. It is claimed *problematically*. [This science] says: given that such and such exists, such and such follows. Thus, science itself consists in an analysis of this presupposition. In this way we achieve some simplicity in the investigation (IV/6, 77).

of the world] (that is, with the reflective awareness [*Reflex*] of this relationship). What concerns us is the analysis of this assertion! How is it possible? What does it presuppose? What is entailed by it, or what follows from it?

(I) The *concept* [is thought of here] in opposition to the world, as a mere image to which nothing at all corresponds and which exhibits itself in consciousness as something to which nothing corresponds. Thus, we are considering the way in which the concept is *absolutely representational* [*absolutbildlich*]. [It is] a *pure, self-sufficient* image, neither a *likeness* [*Abbild*] nor a *copy* [*Nachbild*].

(1) It is not {a likeness or copy} *of* the world whose ground it is supposed to be; [the concept] *is* not [a ground] unless it | *becomes* one. It is not [a ground] merely on account of the fact that *it* exists but rather only if it becomes a ground, and only on account *of the fact that* it becomes [a ground] will it be one. We could consider the world or being of which [the concept] is supposed to be the ground to be the *entire* world or being, to be the sole possible absolute being.[3] (2) Just as little as [the concept is a likeness or copy of the world] is it somehow [a likeness or copy] of a *different* world or being. In that case, the concept would not really be the ground of the world, [at least] not immediately, [since the concept] as such would not be primary. Instead, this different, higher world would be the ground of the lower world by means of the concept and by virtue of the fact that it proceeds through the concept. In this way there would be something that is not posited in the presupposition that we have to analyze. [The original proposition] (α) does not exceed its own scope, is absolute, and therefore is something given that circumscribes the boundaries of our science. It recognizes *concept* and *world* in just this relationship. Therefore, (β) when it speaks of a ground, it means an absolute ground.[4]

Thus, as we already said, being on the basis of the concept is *all* being, and beyond that there is nothing. |

---

3. CAUER: We could [consider] the being that is supposed to be created as all being and as all the world.

4. CAUER: Our presupposition is ABSOLUTE and is given as such, and through it the domain of our science is delimited. [Our science] talks about *concept* and *world* and about a {determinate} relationship [between] {them}. We hold ourselves to this proposition in that {we} do not concern ourselves with what lies beyond it.

(It may well be discovered in philosophy as a whole that the image described in this way is actually a *likeness* of a higher being. What is discovered is that it is the image of God. But the theory of ethics neither can nor should know anything about this. From the point of view occupied by [the theory of ethics, the concept] is not [the image of God]. All that the theory of ethics asserts [is the presupposition described previously], and any different treatment of the sciences is a confusion.[5] The theory of ethics must not know anything about God but rather must consider the concept itself as absolute. This holds in two respects: (1) as a scientific maxim, for the [sake of] the purity of the sciences; and (2) [because] the theory of ethics is not philosophy, | and a philosophy that has this as its highest principle is incomplete. This is what is best in Kant.[6]

StA 271

(2) The concept [is the ground of the world] *in a possible* consciousness. In order to understand this correctly here, [we must think of] the concept as concept, or as image. It must therefore be subsumed under the concept of an image as such and so is more than just an image; [it is] an exemplification or exhibition of [what] an image [is], a determinate, qualitative image constituted in a particular way.[7, 8]

---

5. HALLE: [The theory of ethics] is nothing but the articulation [*Aussprechen*] of this point of view, which is one among five possible points of view (IV/6, 78).

6. HALLE: What is best in Kant is the theory of ethics; he has not gone any further. What is highest for him is the categorical imperative (an important idea, but one that should not be placed at the pinnacle of science). Thus Kant, also, could know nothing of God (IV/6, 78).

7. CAUER: Consciousness must be able to say that what is present is an image (subsumed under the image of an image as such). What is present must therefore be something more—a particular exemplification and exhibition of the image as such—with qualitative content.

8. HALLE: [According to the theory of ethics] the concept is the ground of the world in a possible consciousness. This concept should therefore be a concept for a higher concept of consciousness, a concept that appears as a concept or as an image that can be subsumed within consciousness. Consciousness will be able to say that what is present is an image (subsumed under the image of an image as such). What is present must therefore be more than a concept; it must be the exhibition in intuition or determinate exemplification of an image as such. It must, therefore, have a certain determinate, qualitative content; [it must be] an image constituted in such and such a way, which is expressed in such and such a way (IV/6, 78).

Main comment: [the concept] is, as was stated, a pure and absolute image or idea [*Gesicht*] to which nothing corresponds.[9] Whoever affirms a theory of ethics, morality, etc., affirms this as well and must do so. I have stated the matter in this simple and specific manner so that you understand it once and for all. Spirit [*Geist*] is what primarily and truly exists, from which the world first {follows}. I do not know how someone could ever talk of morality without [making this claim]. Still, this comment will become clearer presently {through what follows}, so I will withhold it.

(II) The concept [is considered] {as} the ground of *the world* or of *being*. The world or being [is considered as] the object of an image, or as *what is copied* [*abgebildete*] in an image that shows itself within consciousness as the image [of this object]. [The image] is something that does not exist if [the world or being] does not exist, though [the world or being] is depicted [*gebildet*] as being capable of existing without this [image]. [The world or being] is the object of an image that is not pure. | (1) [It should be pointed out] that some things are described by me that are not [described] by others (e.g., that being should not be defined holds as a principle [*Grundsatz*] and was the source of all error). Thus, the descriptions likewise sound different. One should not be astonished by the *Wissenschaftslehre*.

(2) Here and in similar sciences one should describe [things] factually; [that is, one should say that] *such and such exists*. In this way the pupil is required only to recognize [the fact] and rediscover it for himself in such a description. The *Wissenschaftslehre* is deductive, and takes up the facts in a different way. | In addition to everything else, it is good to engage with these sciences on the basis of a serious decision [*Beschlossenheit*].

(a) Both concepts, the *pure* and the objective, each carry their characteristics with themselves in immediate

---

9. The term *Gesicht* is usually translated throughout as "idea," following Fichte's own comments in the 1811 *Lectures on the Scholar's Vocation*, where he observes that *Gesicht* is an apt rendering of the Greek *idea* (StA 6). Occasionally, where the German *Idee* occurs in the same sentence, I have translated *Gesicht* more literally as "something that is seen."

consciousness, partly as images in general, and partly with the more precise determinations of being without a relation or being with a relation. They are only possible in opposition to one another, i.e., both [images] are *conceived through one another*.

(b) Being is therefore resolved into its concept, that is, the objective [concept]. It is not definable, nor does it arise in consciousness (in which the grounding of being through the concept is supposed to occur) otherwise than through the concept. One could therefore express the proposition that was set forth [*aufgestellten*] [at the beginning of this lecture] in this way: the pure concept becomes the ground of the objective [concept]. The concept in one sense is the ground of itself in a different sense.

(III) [The concept] is a ground [means that] something *comes to be*, is created absolutely through the concept, namely, *all* being; there is no being [that comes to be] otherwise than through [the concept].[10] In the theory of ethics the world of the concept, of the spirit, is the only primary and true [world]. The [world] of being is merely secondary. Affirm a pure world of the spirit [*Geisteswelt*] and proceed from this as the only true [world]. Whoever does not concede [this world] as primary (moral = spiritual, and in the spirit) is someone for whom the word | morality has no meaning. (This is stated here very simply, and, I think, very clearly; one only understands it correctly if it is taken seriously). [The word "morality"] has no meaning for *Naturphilosophie*; for it, the world is primary and the concept is merely a copy.[11] This is

---

10. CAUER: The concept is the *ground* of the world; thus the world *is created* absolutely through the concept. We could correctly understand the world as all being—then it could be asserted that the concept is the creator of all being.

11. Fichte here refers primarily to Schelling, his erstwhile colleague with whom he had more recently had a bitter dispute. Beginning with *Ideas for a Philosophy of Nature* (1797), Schelling had developed a nonmaterialist, vitalist conception of nature as a necessary supplement to the kind of transcendental idealism Fichte was developing. By the first decade of the nineteenth century, Fichte was openly critical of Schelling's ideas. Partly in response to Fichte's criticisms, Schelling published a brief essay entitled "Presentation of the True Relationship between *Naturphilosophie* and the Improved Fichtean Doctrine" (1806). Fichte's comments in this lecture reflect the acrimonious nature of the dispute.

II/13, 310

StA 274

absolutely opposed to any moral philosophy.[12, 13] Whether | there could be a being other than [the world of the spirit] that is not created through the concept, and | in what sense, is something that we will be led to explain during the course of the analysis.

---

12. [Fichte's marginal note:] But if they [i.e., *Naturphilosophen*] do [affirm morality], {this is} merely an illusion [*Schein*]. The concept [according to *Naturphilosophie*] is the objective concept of the world. The world returns back into itself by way of a detour through the concept. Thus, something appears as though it *exists*, but it is not *morality*. [Mere] *shadows*.

13. HALLE: For *Naturphilosophen* there can be no theory of ethics, nor indeed for philosophers who believe in things-in-themselves. [. . .] How can *Naturphilosophie* pretend to a theory of ethics? For it, the concept is also itself the ground of being. They too say as much. But here they are helping themselves by means of the concept. For them [the concept] is nothing but a likeness and a copy of being, of the given, sensible being of nature. Being everywhere acts efficaciously upon itself and is the ground of itself. In certain cases it takes a detour; it proceeds through the concept of itself in order to then act efficaciously on being. Thus all concepts of morality are also physical (IV/6, 79–80).

Lecture 2

(June 30, 1812)

The proposition [that the concept is the ground of the world] can also be expressed this way: reason, or the concept, is practical. Without this [claim] there is no notion of a theory of ethics. We have actually said more than this in our [assertion that the concept is the] *ground* of all being. It needs to be shown how these expressions relate to one another.[1]

Note: an *ought* {is found} in the first principle [*Grundsatze*] of the theory of right but not in that of the theory of ethics; in the latter [science, the ought] must be derived.[2, 3]

That would be the first point. {It is thus a matter of} simply analyzing the proposition [that] the concept is the ground of the world. However, we added the qualification *with consciousness*. It is precisely only by means of this

---

1. HALLE: (4) The concept is the ground of all being. But how a being prior to morality, in which it finds its domain, {could be constituted} is something that must be disclosed later. Here we know nothing of this. Previously, the presupposition [of the theory of ethics] was expressed thus: *reason or the concept is practical*. We have, at bottom, said nothing more than what this Kantian expression says, as will be shown later (IV/6, 80).

2. CAUER: In the theory of right, at any rate, it is said that the freedom of many ought to subsist alongside [the freedom] of others—because [the theory of right] is subordinate to the theory of ethics.

3. HALLE: In the theory of right it says that the freedom of many *ought* to coexist, since the theory of right is subordinate to the theory of ethics; but the latter is totally self-sufficient. Were there an ought in the theory of ethics it would have to be derived within it; it would have to follow from the basic concept via analysis (IV/6, 80).

addition that the theory of ethics is distinguished from philosophy as a whole, at least with respect to [the philosophy] that we have set forth.

Thus, a new *task* {is posed}: to show this relationship [of concept to world] within the form of consciousness,[4] or, to describe the *consciousness* of the concept's being a ground. {If we wish} to limit ourselves only to the former, then the latter comes to us along with it in this form.

Thus {it is necessary} to analyze this consciousness.

It should be understood that, through assuming this form, the entire relation of being a ground that has been indicated earlier is completely pervaded and further determined [and] receives a completely different characteristic.

Some things may be found in this analysis that you would not have expected here. In order to relieve any disconcertment, you should be mindful that (1) we are here only involving ourselves with the theory of ethics, considering it as if it were all of knowing [*Wissen*], as though outside of it there were no knowing; thus we must consider some things completely and only from this viewpoint, while there is another viewpoint from which they can be considered; and (2) since the theory of ethics occupies a high rank in the series of particular sciences, [such that] above it there is only the theory of religion and below it there are the theories of right and of nature, the views that are derived from [the theory of ethics] might well be in fact the truest, most correct, and deepest, in that its point of view actually justifies the others.

Totally aside from the true goal of establishing a theory of ethics it could happen that an entirely new light could be shed on the truths of the general *Wissenschaftslehre* through these investigations. Where this does occur, I will note it in passing.

To the point: the concept's being a ground in the form *of consciousness*.

General [*comments*]. This relationship of being a ground is such that it carries its reflection with itself. It is more

---

4. HALLE: *Task*. To analyze the consciousness of the causality of the concept for producing the world (IV/6, 80).

correct, precise, and deep [to say that] the being of the relationship and its reflection are one absolutely inseparable unity. In this way we reach the center. Being only really exists in a reflection and as its projection, and the reflection {is} precisely a real [one] that posits being.[5]

Particular [comments].

(1) Something's being a ground, in this case, the concept's [being a ground], is in immediate consciousness (intuition) a transition from nonbeing, i.e., not being a ground, to being, namely, being a ground, causality. As in every case, here too intuition is posited in the genesis of what is intuited; it sees it *coming to be* and originating from nonbeing, and it necessarily assumes being a ground in order to make not being a ground intuitive. [The intuition] is itself the image of something in the *middle*, between both sides of a transition from one thing to another. How it appears to you is something that must be discovered through immediate intuition.

That the concept is intuited as a ground therefore means that it is intuited with the *act* of being a ground. Posit such an act of tearing loose from negation to being posited. *Act* is a very apt expression for that which mediates being and nonbeing, or for transition.

Thus and in this form the concept would intuit the *occurrence* of its being a ground and thereby really make it into an occurrence. What is objectively *intuited* and present would be changed; transition from the noncausality of the concept to causality.[6]

(2) There is something higher that should be introduced by this first [point, namely, that] the concept is a ground absolutely *through itself*, in accord with the presupposition [of the theory of ethics], otherwise it would not be a *ground*. It belongs within being a ground that [what is a ground] is

---

5. CAUER: Morality is not a thing-in-itself but rather something within consciousness and a determination of consciousness—though not an empty image but rather something upon which consciousness as a whole rests.

6. HALLE: Hence what is intuited comes to be something that is in flux [*Fließenden*], an occurrence. The intuition [or] passive image is torn from one state to another and intuited [in this process] (IV/6, 81).

so out of itself, from itself, and immediately through itself, just as everyone who understands the concept of a ground assumes.

[That] the [concept] is intuited as being a ground through itself means that it is intuited as something that in itself transitions from indeterminacy with respect to being a ground to determinacy with respect [to being a ground]. Indeed, [the concept is intuited] as transitioning in this way not through some other thing (which would not be a transitioning) but absolutely through itself. Thus, [the concept is intuited] as *determining* itself with respect to being a ground.[7]

The concept therefore becomes, in the immediate consciousness of its being a ground, something self-determining (though not with respect to the content of the concept, for this is simply assumed; rather [this holds only] with respect to being a ground)—as something that, absolutely through itself, tears itself loose from the possibility of being a ground to its actuality, as something absolutely self-creating with respect to this reality. Now let this self-determination be once more the ground of the objective transitioning of whose occurrence I talked about earlier under heading (1).

{Now the} precise analysis. I enjoin you to participate in it and arrive at your own conviction of its correctness. The concept is intuited as being a ground, i.e., as transitioning from inactivity and inefficacy to efficacy. This is an occurrence through which inefficacy and efficacy are linked, and in it the intuition is passive in being torn loose from the former to the latter via the point of transition. Once again, the concept is the *ground* of this occurrence through its absolute self-determination to efficacy, for it is the absolutely creative elevating of mere possibility into actuality. This [second] transition, which is entirely different [from the first], is also intuited. Both of the chief parts of the intuition are once again linked as ground and consequent, like what is inferred from what is absolutely seen [*wie ersehenes aus*

---

7. HALLE: [. . .] this self-determination would again be the ground of something objective, the ground of an occurrence, as its original, inner vital drive [*Lebenstrieb*] (IV/6, 82).

einem absolut gesehenen].⁸ The consciousness as a whole is fivefold; it has two chief parts, each of which is [in turn] a transition that has two parts, and [the whole] is linked through a fifth member.⁹

[In this way] an absolute creativity of consciousness, or of the image [becomes apparent]. [This provides] an example of the doctrine that I lectured on yesterday in the logical [course] (Lecture on the transformation of original appearance through self-appearance and its form).¹⁰

This is the true center of intuition: actual being a ground. What it really provides is the mere *possibility* of being a ground, a *terminus a quo* for the *actuality* of being a ground. Remember this well. We will next cast our attention on the *possibility* that is freely brought about through sheer visibility.¹¹

---

8. CAUER: Both parts are associated as ground and consequent—as what is inferred and what is absolutely seen. Thus, the entire consciousness is something fivefold, as all consciousness must be.

9. HALLE: That the concept is intuited as a ground means [that it is intuited] as transitioning from inactivity to activity. This is an occurrence for the passive intuition that is torn loose along with it; and through the intuition efficacy is linked to inefficacy. The concept is the ground of the fact that there is such [an occurrence] through its self-determination to efficacy, which is the absolute creation of actuality out of possibility. This inner transition, which is something different from the external one, is also intuited. However, both (the inner [transition] of self-determination and the external [transition] of the occurrence) are once again linked, like ground and consequent, like what is inferred from something absolutely seen. The entire consciousness has two eyes, each of which again has two parts united through one in the middle. Thus [it is] something fivefold, as all consciousness must be (IV/6, 82).

10. See GA II/14, 90–93.

11. CAUER: Now intuition is in the center—inherent in being a ground itself—but now it must be shown that the whole relationship presupposes the possibility of being a ground.

Lecture 3

(July 1, 1812)

II/13, 313

A comment for the sake of clarifying what follows as well as the entire present investigation: We have said that the *concept*, the concept itself and not something else in its stead, is a ground. One can rest assured that this formula, in the analysis of which our entire science is supposed to consist, is not said in a merely metaphorical or figurative manner but rather must be understood quite literally. Common sense balks at this literal sense; it does not understand it | and fails to hear it, putting in its place something completely different. The concept is a ground. Now [common sense] thinks it is evident that [the concept] is not [a ground] immediately, for a concept is after all a dead idea (should an idea, as Kant once asked very ingenuously [*naiv*], itself think or even act?).[1] Rather [it is assumed] that [the concept is a ground] by means of a thinking substance endowed with force, as in human beings. Whoever wants to can certainly {construe} [the claim] this way and in so doing misunderstand it crudely. Indeed, this is how one has taken the Kantian formula that reason is practical. In this

---

1. Fichte is most likely referring to the following passage in Kant's 1786 essay, "What Does It Mean to Orient Oneself in Thinking?": "Spinozism speaks of thoughts which themselves think, and thus of an accident that simultaneously exists for a subject: a concept that is not to be found in the human understanding and moreover cannot be brought into it" (Königlichen Preußischen [later Deutschen] Akademie der Wissenschaften, ed., *Kants gesammelte Schriften* [Berlin: Georg Reimer (later Walter De Gruyter), 1900–], henceforth cited as AA 8:143n).

way, [the claim] is deprived of meaning. (It was not always entirely clear to Kant how it should be understood).

Now if, in addition, it is also posited (as in our case) [that the concept is a ground] in consciousness, then the misinterpretation is entirely complete. In consciousness—*only I* possess that; thus [the concept] occurs in my consciousness | {as a ground}; [the concept] is [a ground] through me, by means of some I.

But what if the premise of this argument were something fundamentally mistaken that allowed [this false] notion to arise in the first place? What if it were not the I that possessed consciousness but rather consciousness that possessed the I and that produced it out of itself? [This is] an idea at which the *Wissenschaftslehre* is not in the least bit dismayed. What if the first principle of the theory of ethics that we have set forth were one of the points at which one could grasp this in the most compelling way? Would one then be less hasty to discard the entire doctrine that we have in mind? What if it were the concept of which we are speaking that itself assumed the form of consciousness, and in it the form of an I, of a thinking substance endowed with force? Would we not have to first of all see how it did so, how it underwent this transformation, and thus take the formula literally from the beginning?

This is what I mean when I always say that philosophy is pure thinking. Yet people usually do not hear that, and therefore they do not understand philosophy; that is, whatever one might say to them, they straightaway grasp [what has been said] in immediate forms of intuition. [These immediate forms] are facts to them, as the present example makes clear. [They proceed this way,] rather than avoiding these [forms] from the beginning as they should, in order to enter into their genesis and to see how pure ideas are clothed [*eingekleidet*] by them. It is precisely this insight in which philosophy consists. |

[All this is said] in a general way. Now to the point.

Self-consciousness of the concept in its causality = immediate inner intuition of absolute self-determination with respect to causality, to which corresponds in an immediate way causality in objective intuition, which results from [absolute self-determination]. This is the pith and center described in its fivefold nature: the *fact* of consciousness.²

StA 280 Now, I say | further that a consciousness like the one described here presupposes a number of things:

It presupposes for its own possibility several different elements that it therefore brings along with itself through its absolute being, through the absolute taking up of the causality of the concept in the form of consciousness. What are these presupposed or indirectly posited elements?—For the present [we are talking about] elements *in plurali*. Later on we will trace them back to a unity. Our present task is subordinate to the question about the form of consciousness as such.

(1) As per the declaration of consciousness that the concept absolutely determines itself with respect to actual causality, elevating the mere possibility [of causality] to actuality—I may not always add this formulation, but I expect you to do so. It therefore requires such a determination {of the concept}, and without it, through its mere being, it is not yet a ground. Through its mere being [the concept] is indeed a potential, [a potential] to become such a ground through absolute self-determination. Thus, *through its mere being in the form of consciousness* [the concept] is *life*—as such, a formal life that can become an actual, self-expressing life absolutely through itself. [It is] an absolutely *free* life that can express itself or not. This is meant in a precise sense. The yes or no lies in the fact that through mere being it is only a *formal* life, a potential for self-determination and nothing more.³

The concept is synthesized with life and thus made concrete by means of this element of the presupposition; by virtue of [this element the concept] is permeated by [life], becoming an absolutely living concept [or] a life that conceptualizes in accord with the form of the concept [*ein begreifendes, nach der Form eines Begriffs einhergehendes*
StA 281 *Leben*]. |

---

2. CAUER: This is the genuine fact of consciousness. This is how it is in immediate life and in the movement of seeing.

3. HALLE: Upon what does self-determination depend? Life is absolutely free to the highest power in relation to both determining itself and not {determining itself} (IV/6, 84).

(a) I said that the elements that are presupposed by the causality of the concept by way of a possible fact of consciousness would later on be capable of being comprehended as a unity. Here, I will only recall that this unity, and within it the entire form of the unity of consciousness of a concept, has been discovered; [this unity] is just the taking up of the [concept] into the form of vitality [*Lebendigkeit*] and the synthesis with [this form]. For the purposes of an intuition of the absolute causality of the concept, the form of consciousness adds | only life; this may just as easily follow immediately from causality.

(b) One of the main points of the *Wissenschaftslehre* {can be} made clear {here}. {The question may arise of how} a merely formal life acquires a determinate quality, and whence [it does so]. {How} is {appearance} not appearance as such but rather the appearance of something that is determined through itself, [that is,] the {appearance} of the absolute or of God? What is discovered here is that {life} acquires this content through the absolute content of the pure concept, which is made concrete along with this. [However, the content] of a concept may well only acquire its conceptual form [*Begriffform*] through the self-comprehension of appearance; in that case, the qualitative content [of the concept] remains pure, as a determination of pure life. It is difficult for me to tell you what benefits would accrue for your clear understanding of the *Wissenschaftslehre* were you to comprehend this.[4,5]

---

4. CAUER: Demonstrating in a determinate way how generative life acquires a qualitative content in consciousness takes no small effort in a philosophical investigation. [Put differently, it is difficult to demonstrate] how the life that is being considered by philosophy is not life as such but rather a determinate life. What is discovered here is that life is determined through the absolute content of the pure concept and obtains its [own] content in this manner. The theory of ethics does not address how things stand in general with the concept [*Wie es überhaupt zum Begriff komme geht der Sittenlehre nichts an*]. In the *Wissenschaftslehre* it is shown why the ground takes on the form of the concept.

5. HALLE: I said that some of the main points of the *Wissenschaftslehre* would be made clear here, and this is one of those instances. It is difficult to show how a qualitative content enters the form of consciousness, or even how the life that is being considered by philosophy is not appearance as such but rather a determinate appearance, the appearance of something that exists, [namely,] of the Absolute. The question is how a content occurs within this life. What is discovered here is that life is determined through the absolute content of the pure concept, and appearance obtains this content through being made concrete in an absolute way with the pure concept (IV/6, 84–85).

(2) The life of the concept determines itself absolutely. For what? For *actual causality*, which occurs immediately as a result of this self-determination and along with it in a transition from the potential for such causality to its actuality. Thus, the potential for actual | causality is assumed. It is posited through the mere being of the concept. Life is just the possibility of being a real principle; hence, it is a real principle in a *formal* sense.[6] That is, it is not actually a [principle] simply by virtue of being one formally; rather, it is capable of becoming a [principle] through sheer self-determination.

---

6. CAUER: (Something can be called a principle in two ways. (1) If something can determine itself to be a principle, then the word is used *formally*. (2) If something *is* in fact a principle in actual life, then the word is taken dynamically [*energisch*].)

Lecture 4

(July 2, 1812)

It is important to understand more clearly than is usually done what a real principle might be. {It is commonly said [that a principle is]} the ground of a being, of the world, etc. We start with this. But if this being a ground is actualized [*vollendet*], what would the new thing that previously did not exist be? An impression [*Abdruk*] of the concept and of its efficacy would arise outside of the concept and its life, {something} that previously was not present insofar as the concept was merely within itself in an interior way. What does it mean [to say that something is] outside *of itself*? That [it exists] in a merely passive, objective intuition. {Thus we return to} the previous formula, namely, that the concept in one of its forms (the pure [form]) is the ground of itself in a different form (the objective [form]), a form that is regarded as a mere likeness. That the concept is the ground of itself means that it deposits its inner being outside of itself in an objective being [*er sezt außer sich ab, in einem objektiven Seyn sein inneres Seyn*]. That it has actualized a potential to be a ground means that [the concept] has the potential, *inter alia*, to set down an image outside of itself that bears the seal of its inner essence. It is an absolutely free, real, and objective power.[1]

In sum, a life = a potential for determining itself internally and, as a result of this self-determination, to be the

---

1. CAUER: The concept in [its] pure form deposits itself in its external, objective form. The external and internal being of the concept are only different in the form of intuition.

ground in an absolutely creative way of a being outside of itself.

(3) Please note that up to this point we have described what happens to consciousness on account of the form of the concept's being a ground in general; we have completely abstracted away from the fact that this concept is always something qualitatively determined. | This [concept] is supposed to be a ground and [thus is supposed to] be provided with a living, self-determining, and free power to create being. Now what follows from this? This {will} be the question henceforth; in this way [we can] completely resolve the main task regarding the form of consciousness.

Obviously, it is the case that the power that is being assumed does not determine itself to be a ground in general of that for which it is somehow supposed to be [a ground], such that only the form of action belongs to self-determination. [In that case] the power would only be formally free, whereas what results from freedom would fall under a different law. You are familiar with the fact that such merely formal freedom occurs in all reflection; the seeing that is constrained frees itself, and the seeing that results falls under a law. Is it also true in the present case that the life that is constrained with respect to its potential merely frees itself through absolute self-determination, while what results from it falls under a different law? At least up to this point it looks as though this is the case. Our presentation so far leaves just such a residual idea.

How do things stand? A determinate concept is a ground; life determines itself to causality in accord with [the concept]. A completely determined product = a, the negation of every possible not-a, belongs within the self-determination and hence within the action. It first of all follows from this that the power is materially and qualitatively *free* in both respects, [namely,] as a principle of being and as [a principle] of its own inner self-determination. [It is] *infinitely determinable* with respect to the production of a certain intended effect. (Stated clearly, the qualitative {is} an organic unity of a manifold. If this manifold is different, then it {is} totally different. {This power must therefore be} a power to absolutely determine any manifold. This {would be} the first subordinate [point]). Nevertheless, a good deal follows from this. The organization and articulation of the human body is ultimately based on this principle. This [is noted] in passing.[2] |

(4) There must be a paradigm [*Vorbild*] of the intended product that is [itself] completely united to and melded with self-determining freedom—[call it] *a*. {This paradigm would have to be} under the sway of or in the possession of freedom, of my I, so that the power is determined in accord with it. This is important; it is the *nervus decidendi* [crux of the decision]. To use a common | expression that only here takes on a clear meaning: freedom must possess this paradigm [*die Freiheit muß dieses Vorbild haben*]. This paradigm belongs absolutely, and in a thoroughly determined way, within the pure, absolute concept that was previously presupposed. Hence, as the paradigm of self-determination and action, it would have to be in the possession of the free power. The free power itself, as such (here we arrive at the goal) must construct it and be its synthetic unity, since it is supposed to construct self-determination and action by means of the real power and in accord with [the paradigm].

I want to lend you a helping hand so that this is grasped in a precise way, for it is important for the theory of ethics and for philosophy in general to be clear about this point, and this is the right occasion [for this]. False [*Nichtwahr*].[3] Action is just an organic unity of a manifold, and the power is what determines and directs this *manifold* according to the unity that the power already intuits and surveys.[4] Posit that $\alpha, \beta, \gamma, \delta$ belong to this manifold. It is clear that the real power would have to determine itself [to move] from α directly to β, and never to some possible non-β; likewise from β to γ, and not to a non-γ, and so forth. It could only

---

2. CAUER: Qualitative determinacy is without a doubt the organic unity of a manifold—were some individual within it different, it would be a different unity. The power must therefore be determined with respect to such a manifold and thus [with respect] to such elements, precisely as they belong within the concept.

3. In light of the corresponding passage from Halle, it would seem that this word belongs to a thought that Fichte did not develop further.

4. HALLE: The action of production is an organic unity of a manifold, and the free power is what determines this manifold according to the unity that this power already surveys intuitively (IV/6, 87).

do this in accord with a paradigm in which the α, β, etc., that are supposed to be produced in succession through action would already be complete [*schon vollendet*] and comprehended as a unity.[5] [The real power] would therefore be the synthetic unity of these elements in two respects. [First], ideally, in an image, and this image would be complete; [second], *in a real way*, as the productive force of an image in being, where the latter is directed in its succession by the former.[6] {Thus [the power] comes apart} into a duality. A higher view would be required for it to comprehend itself as this synthetic unity | in both the image and the real, efficacious action, to the extent that the latter is supposed to be determined by the former within this higher view. In a word, [the real power] becomes a power into which an eye is inserted, [an eye] that accompanies it evermore. The absolute identity of seeing and of life is an I; thus, the life of a concept that has causality necessarily takes on the form of an I in consciousness and is transformed into the causality [of an I].

The true character of the I, of freedom, of intelligence [*Geistigkeit*] is [that of] a power into which an eye is inserted. Anyone who is able to furnish himself with a correct, vivid image of this and to retain it, and who knows it as the basis of all his judgments of things of this sort, has accomplished a great deal. Sight accompanies the power. It is immediately visible as it flows forth across α, β, γ; it *guides* the power; it sees the path that it must describe; {it sees} β while it is still enacting α and so forth. It *determines* [*the power*] through its *guidance*. In just the way that the dynamic [*kräftige*] and vital sight [*Sehe*] moves itself through α to β, the real power follows it immediately, for the power

---

5. HALLE: α α
   IMAGE A β   REAL EFFICACIOUS ACTION B β
   γ γ

B/α β γ The image is complete. Thus in B a synthetic unity of the manifold.

A/α β γ The efficacious action is successive; it is directed in a succession always in accord with the image, in which there is no succession (IV/6, 88).

6. CAUER: The image is complete—efficacious action is directed successively in accord with the complete paradigm. Both must once again be comprehended as identical in a higher image.

II/13, 318 just is what the sight is, only in the real form of life. The claim that | the concept is immediately a ground means this and should be taken in this way: [namely, that] sight is immediately and through itself creative life; reality is in fact *sighted* [*hingesehen*]. I say it is sighted without the application of some different organ. [Rather,] it is sighted as reality, not as a mere image; at the same time it is reality for a different, objective form of intuition.[7]

---

7. HALLE: What one calls physical force is an intellectual activity [*Intelligiren*]. Intellectual activity appears within the theory of ethics as something that is not a copy and thus not a paradigm. This is the pure ground (IV/6, 88).

Lecture 5

(July 7, 1812)

StA 286

{The} analysis {was} easy [*leicht*]. {The} concept {is} a ground in consciousness.[1] (1) {It} becomes a life, a life as a real ground in the world of objective seeing. (2) {But it is} a | *determinate* concept, an ideal and real potential at one and the same time.[2] An I: a power into which an eye is inserted, which is inseparable from it; the power of an I; the characteristic of the I and of intelligence. Sight accompanies, guides, and determines the power. {Thus} self-determination = a self-transformation of the merely ideal principle into a *real* [principle], i.e., into one that is absolutely creative in an objective seeing. (One form of the concept [is transformed] into another.)

Analyzed more precisely:

The main product of the form of consciousness is a formal principle, i.e., life in the sense of a potential, [that is] a stable being that is at rest, posited in consciousness, something that is purely intuited. [This life is] something objective that is present on the credit of intuition [*auf den Kredit der Anschauung*], in an objective form of intuition. [It is] a mere potential that is immediately intuited as the ground of the world, as being objective or as existing. Yet it

---

1. HALLE: In consciousness, life is introduced to the concept, a life that contains a completely new world within itself (IV/6, 88).

2. [Fichte's marginal note:] The I possesses the concept that is being presupposed in an ideal way and constructs it in an ideal way. An ideal, representing [*bildendes*] life, is added to the concept. [The concept] becomes a ground. Thus, it is a real life in the form of an I (StA 286).

is entirely shapeless. The form of objective consciousness, i.e., some given being, exists but is nothing other than the I, which has no objective shape at all, but rather is supposed to be a mere principle for an objective being that is anticipated.[3] Now if this principle actualizes its freedom and becomes a ground, then another objective being arises outside of the I, which is its creator. [The I] is the creator of the world and by means of it so is the concept.

In this way the objective intuition of a given being occurs in two distinct spheres. [The first] is that of the I as a mere principle of all objectivity without any further objectivity [of its own], in that it is the form of consciousness of the concept as ground. [The second is] that of a not-I, outside of the I, which I must be produced by means of the I as the life of the concept. To this extent objective consciousness depends [on the I], both with respect to the fact *that* it exists as such and with respect to *what* is contained in it. I ({This is a} doctrine that is, on the one hand, essential to the theory of ethics and, on the other hand, sheds light on consciousness as a whole and on philosophy, while the true point of view may indeed arise at this point [*sich ergeb{en} dürfte*]. (1) Absolutely pure seeing is the ground of objective [seeing]; (2) this is true in two senses, i.e., partly in that [pure seeing] enters consciousness as this ground as such, {as} an objective intuition of the I, and partly in that it becomes an actual ground. {The} not-I as a product of and copy of the I, and by means of it of the pure concept.)

An I has been discovered to be the stable, fixed life of the concept, the point of unification for its life. This is the genuine point of view for the theory of ethics. From now on {we must} therefore learn from and analyze the I that has been deduced and cognized from this point of view.

(1) We have seen that the I possesses the concept, [which] is that which appears subjectively in it, and is the synthetic unity of a manifold through its mere being, to the extent that it is only the life of the concept. However, just in case this does actually occur, [the I] must become a

---

3. HALLE: Objective being is set down [*niedergelegt*] here in a noumenon (IV/6 89).

ground in accordance [with the concept] and {must} absolutely determine itself through itself; moreover, [the I] does not {become a ground} through its mere being.[4]

The synthesis of the concept with absolute self-determination as a fact is called a willing [*ein Wollen*]. The potential for absolute self-determination in relation to a concept [is called] a will [*Willen*] or the faculty of will [*Willensvermögen*] as such. Therefore, the I is capable of willing. (For the sake of greater clarity: Is this act of will [*WillensAkt*] an intuition or a thought? There is absolutely no manifold in its inner being; it | is absolute actualization, without any obstruction, which traverses a manifold. It is a complete, absolute unity. The I also knows without any mediation that this is what it is. [The act of will] is the pure interpenetration of being and image, and to that extent it is a *thought*. But, within intuition, [the act of will] is the absolute transition from one standpoint (the ideal) to its opposite, and thus it is the synthesis of a duality. To this extent, [the act of will] is an *intuition*. One could call it an intellectual intuition.

Thus, the I that has been described can *will*, and it is free either to will or not to will. If one wants to call this freedom of the will, then one may indeed do so, though {this must be} understood correctly. [It must be understood] in this way: the I is not free either to possess the concept or not to possess it; it possesses it through its mere being and is merely the ideal life [of the concept]. Nevertheless [the I] is free; that is, [whether or not] it determines itself to be a ground depends upon its absolute self-determination within its already given being. The addition of this self-determination is willing; it is therefore free as such to will or not to will. Its being is indifferent with respect to willing | and it is up to it whether it does so or not. Not willing means that [the I] remains in a bare state of ideal contemplation and construction, and it is capable of doing so.

But in no way does this mean that the will is *qualitatively free* to will in general and, thence, [to will] this or

---

4. HALLE: This I of ours possesses the concept; the I is the subjective synthetic unity of the manifold in the concept that intuits and constructs; and the I is this [synthetic unity] simply through its mere being (IV/6, 90).

something else. For (1) *will* and *freedom* are only the transition from ideal to real, from the state of a concept to its realization. Freedom just is the causality of a concept—a proposition that admittedly has not been well understood before now but that Kant already demonstrated perfectly well.[5] (2) Were the will | qualitatively free, that would have to mean that there would be multiple concepts whose ground it could be. But, according to the presupposition [made at the beginning of the lecture course] this is impossible, since a determinate | concept is given, beyond which there are no more and whose ground it is or not; in that case it is not a ground at all and does not will at all.

[These comments] pass over [*sezt . . . hinweg*] a host of errors that accrue to this much-discussed concept of the freedom of the will. |

(Here we are completely abstracting away from the domain of the empirical, i.e., of an objective being that is not produced via freedom. For us, the I in its entirety is just the formative, dynamic life of the pure concept; we do not recognize some other I. The extent to which, by taking this course, we have done well by the purity and comprehensibility of our science will become increasingly apparent. Whoever {mingles} the domain of the empirical at this point with the theory of the will may perhaps say that there are two concepts in this case, [namely,] that which is given by the selfish natural drive and the pure [concept]. Self-determination is free to follow one or the other, and in this way the will is qualitatively free. There is a freedom of choice between the selfish and unselfish drives, as is commonly, but erroneously, said. To this I reply that this [view] omits the fact that in the empirical domain and under the dominion of the drive there is no willing, | no freedom, and no self-determination at all but rather only determination

---

5. The editors of StA excerpt several long passages from Fichte's 1798 theory of ethics, as well as from Kant's *Critique of Pure Reason* and *Critique of Practical Reason*, in which this claim about willing as the causality of a concept is discussed in more detail.

through a factual law.⁶ Thus, what [those who expound this view] allege in their claim is void and our assertion stands).

To repeat: (1) the will [is] the synthesis of absolute self-determination with the ideal possession of the concept. Is it a *fact*? It would seem so. The essence of this {willing} consists in its appearing as a fact. {At bottom, however, it is} posited through self-consciousness. [The will is, therefore,] the absolute coincidence of ideal and real, the only immediate fact of this inseparability, and so the point of unification of both worlds (from which all the relations between these two [worlds] must be deduced and to which [they must all] be traced back in any rigorous philosophy).

(2) The I is free to will or not; in the latter case [it is free] to endure in a mere state of ideality. There is no other willing besides that which accords with the concept. {This} is the main point.

---

6. CAUER: Whoever mixes in the *empirical I* and the objective empirical world at this point would perhaps say that there are two wills—one [that proceeds] on the basis of the pure concept, the other [that proceeds] on the basis of the natural drive, and in this way the will is qualitatively free. Unfortunately, this completely overlooks the fact that nothing is ever *willed* in the empirical domain—the empirical I is subordinate to the law of nature. Freedom and willing in the empirical domain are only an image of moral willing, which are supposed to arise later on. Here, we are not talking about the empirical domain at all.

Lecture 6

(July 8, 1812)

To continue:[1, 2]

(1) It has been made completely clear that the I, with its ideal life and its real, objective power, is nothing other than the life of the concept that is itself endowed with causality [*begründenden*]. It is not something in itself, nor [is it] a life of its own; rather, it is only the life and the power of this concept. Admittedly, the concept as such carries with it only its ideal life, | but not its real *effect*. The freedom of the I exists in order for this [real effect] to be produced. Hence, the I, regarded as free and self-sufficient (which it only is as the power of self-determination), exists for the sake of | furnishing the concept with its causality. This is the vocation that defines it, the purpose of its existence: it *ought* to will.

Nervus probandi [crux of the argument]. A free and self-sufficient I is posited through the concept's being a ground and for its sake. If the concept were not to become a ground by means of [the I], then [the I] would be posited in vain; [that is,] positing [the I] would not be able to fulfill the intention behind it.

---

1. CAUER: Will = SYNTHESIS of self-determination with the ideal concept. It is the origin of all FACTICITY and of OBJECTIVE consciousness. Willing is never without consciousness, and the consciousness of willing posits the act of willing. The will is thus the genuine point of unification of both worlds.

2. HALLE: We provide a description of willing because we see it coming into being. Will = SYNTHESIS of self-determination with the ideal concept. It is the origin of all FACTICITY and of OBJECTIVE consciousness. Willing appears as a fact and is the original fact (IV/6, 91).

(Here is the original locus for the production of the concepts of end, intention, defining vocation, ought, and the like. Clear knowledge about [these] concepts is usually lacking. Here we see [these concepts] come into being. An ideal being (a concept to which nothing corresponds) precipitates [*absezt*] itself and is transformed into an objective and real being and thus becomes the principle of something corresponding to it. (1) Ideal being precipitates itself absolutely into the *real*. The I is just the expression of or proxy of the concept; [the I exists] in order to provide [the concept] with something that it is not capable of on its own. {The I is thus} in a real sense what the [concept] is in an ideal sense. [The concept] comes into being only through this depositing precipitation [*Absetzung*]. It is in fact something that is *aimed at* [*abgesehen*], selected, and attended to [*heraus{-} und hingesehen*]. (2) The ground and meaning of this selective attention {is} that it creates the corresponding thing; the meaning of aiming at something is what is intended.[3] The difficulty is not the construction of such a concept in thought, but rather understanding that such a [concept] must be constructed so that it absolutely possesses its reality as well as a relationship to something that corresponds to it. Of course, one can only see this from the point of view where one conceives of the image as in fact what is primary and original, as the ground of the world. In that case, the relationship is obvious. Such a concept can never be comprehended by someone for whom being is primary, i.e., a *Naturphilosoph*.)[4, 5]

---

3. HALLE: The concept is the ground of the world; thus the ideal creates the real. We have discovered this through a detour. What the concept is as a mere image, the I is in a real way as a dynamic image; what the concept is [as] dead, the I is in a living way (IV/6, 92).

4. CAUER: Here, for the first time, the particular concepts of *an end*, of an *ought*, are produced. We have discovered a pure concept to which nothing corresponds transforming itself into a real principle that is supposed to create what corresponds to it.—The I is the expression and proxy of the concept. The I is in a real way what the concept is in an ideal way. The I is thus viewed on the basis of a seeing; the sense or target of the view is a life, namely, that the I creates what corresponds to the concept. The I is the living causality of the concept. If we connect both, then the concept must be posited as a principle and the I as what results from the principle. Therefore, the I must be thought of purely as something that is the result of a principle. This being a ground must be thought of together with the I in a unity—the I *ought*—in this way the concept of an *end* acquires its meaning.

5. HALLE: The concept of an end thus expresses the absolute being a ground of the intellectual with respect to the nonintellectual (IV/6, 92).

(2) The I *ought* to will in accord with the concept that is assumed [at the beginning of this lecture course]. This *ought* is the inner essence and meaning of its existence. (The existence of the I is itself merged into a concept; this {is} its qualitative content; existence is only the comprehension of this concept in an objective consciousness.)[6]

That *we* have understood this is not that important [*Das haben so eben* wir *eingesehen, worauf nicht viel ankommt*]. It is [however] important for the objective presentation of a theory of ethics to know whether and to what extent the I that has been derived must itself understand this point from this perspective.

My answer is yes. The proof is decisive for the correct understanding of the essence of morality. A sharper distinction and synopsis is required. This would be a difficulty, though one that is [resolved] quite briefly and simply. | (1) The causality of the concept, by itself, and not something else in its stead, is supposed to come to consciousness. Hence it is posited, and we must analyze this claim. The causality [of the concept], actually and in fact, not simply the mere demand for causality or drive for causality, etc. (2) Now the concept is actually and in fact only a ground in that it precipitates [*im Absetzen*] the I into this determination. (3) *This* being a ground, {the} absolute determination of the I or the ought, must therefore really enter consciousness. It must enter [consciousness] as the ground of the next succeeding element, i.e., of self-determination or willing. Otherwise, the concept itself has not entered consciousness as being a ground. {Therefore,} in order to will it and bring it to pass, the I must be conscious to itself of its determination as the ground of its existence. It must be conscious to itself that it has willed as a result of this insight, otherwise consciousness is not consciousness of the concept as immediate ground but rather of something else. |

Once again, the concept's being a ground has the following elements, in this order: {first,} the concept precipitates itself into an ideal image of itself alongside a real but free power of actualization; second, this element must itself once more cohere as a ground with the succeeding [element], i.e.,

---

6. CAUER: The I merges into the concept of the end or of the ought—the self-sufficient (objective) existence of (the ought) is only the construal of the intellectual.

the self-determination of the free power or willing. That this being a ground enters consciousness means that all of these elements, located in the order set forth here, enter into consciousness.

Lecture 7

(July 9, 1812)[1]

StA 295

II/13, 324

Two things follow [from what has been said]. (1) The assumed concept enters immediately into consciousness through its being with the additional demand on the I that it *ought* [to do something] (with the accompanying characteristic feature of a categorical imperative, to help myself to Kant's apt designation). For in fact and in truth this concept is the ground of an I. | On account of the fact that [the concept] is a ground, a *real* ground, the I is simply actualized by it. Thus *it exists*. Now the being a ground [of the concept] must enter into consciousness; therefore, this ought | must necessarily enter into [consciousness], and it does so just as certainly as the concept is causally efficacious.

---

1. The text for Lectures 7 and 8 presents some difficulties, in that both the Cauer and Halle transcripts include material under Lecture 7 (July 9) that Fichte's manuscript, reproduced in GA II/13 and in StA, places under Lecture 8 (July 10) (specifically, material corresponding to StA 298–299; II/13, 325–326). Moreover, the transcripts do not completely agree with one another. Halle begins Lecture 8 (July 10) with material corresponding to StA 299, whereas Cauer locates the same material in Lecture 7 (July 9) and begins Lecture 8 (July 10) with the heading "consequences and additions" (StA 300; II/13, 327). It would seem that some of the material indicated in Fichte's manuscript as intended for Lecture 8 was actually delivered in Lecture 7, but the disagreement between the transcripts precludes certainty about precisely what was included. The way in which Cauer ends Lecture 7 seems more natural than does the ending in Halle. Accordingly, I will follow Cauer in dividing the lectures at the heading "consequences and additions," locating the material on StA 300–303; II/13, 326–328 in Lecture 8.

Addition (1). We previously made a distinction between what exists in the I that here comes to be through its mere being and that for which a self-determination within its given being is required. With respect to the former {we found} that [the I] possesses the concept; it is a free synthetic unity that accords with its content. Now [the concept] appears, and it is accompanied by and pervaded by the character of an ought; in this way it is absolutely *unified*, likewise through mere being without anything more appearing in consciousness with the help of the I. This is [said] in the interest of total clarity.[2]

[Addition] (2). The concept, which is determinate in itself, bears this formal characteristic. In Kant it sometimes looks as though this concept is a categorical imperative and with that is complete [*u. damit vollendet*].[3] Indeed, this is how it has been understood on nearly every occasion (it may have been difficult for Kant to communicate how he himself thought about it). This is completely wrong; indeed, if one looks at it closely, it is totally meaningless.[4] On a formal definition that is quite correct; it would thus be the task of philosophy to think of a real theory of ethics, to furnish each empty concept with a content; | indeed, since it appeared, the *Wissenschaftslehre* has posed itself this task and applied itself to it. Of course, the bare theory of ethics can say nothing more about this content than that this concept is not an empty and merely formal categorical imperative. What it might be is something about which each person must be referred to his own moral consciousness. It is the theory of God (or the *Wissenschaftslehre*), which occupies a higher [level than the theory of ethics] that first shows [that the concept is] the image of God. Kant arrived at his view of

---

2. HALLE: According to KANT it emerges along with an absolute postulate of its being (IV/6, 94).

3. Fichte likely has in mind a passage from the *Critique of Practical Reason* in which Kant claims that only a formal principle can be the supreme principle of morality (AA 5:41).

4. CAUER: This is, however, entirely false; the concept is determined in itself.

the matter because he did not discover the principle of the theory of ethics on the path of speculation and deduction but rather empirically, in his own elevated moral consciousness.

(2) {The claim} that the will must regard itself as motivated [*begründet*] by means of the *ought* = {the claim that} the I must discover itself as willing completely and absolutely [just] because it ought, for *this reason* [alone] (not for some other [reason]; another [reason] must not even be considered here).[5] This *must* be the case as a matter of analytical necessity if the concept is supposed to enter [consciousness] as a ground. More clearly, a new intervening element occurs here. The concept is not immediately the ground of willing, for real life is *free* in relation to willing and is an absolutely creative point of origin. But the will is also supposed not to be an absolutely creative point of origin but rather a principle. In between steps the concept of the ought, of absolute *determination*. The appearance or *image* of the essence of the *concept becomes* a self-determination.

The unfolding consequences of the concept's being a ground include the fact that the concept, conceived of in the form of absolute being, becomes the ground of an *I* absolutely through itself. That is, [the concept becomes the ground] of a likeness and expression of itself in an objective form of consciousness. In this I and in its mere being and essence it is equally the subjective-objective image of itself, as concept, with the addition that the I is determined to will it (an image along with the determination of the I in the image). This image of its determination is supposed to become its *actual* determinacy. (Once again, the ideal and real stand in relation to one another as ground and consequent, principle and what results from a principle. This happens here such that they immediately have one and the same object, the I, as their point of unification. The *image* of determination is supposed to become the *actual*

---

5. HALLE: However, the theory of ethics is indeed an image of moral consciousness. Morality enters your consciousness when the consciousness is of the causality of the concept. We are depicting such [a consciousness] (IV/6, 94).

being; the image is supposed to make itself into a *being* immediately and through itself. Image and being, however, are only distinguished here in a positive manner, as are *not [being a] principle* and *[being a] principle*.)[6, 7]

It follows that, if the concept is to occur as a ground, this must occur in consciousness. [*The I*] *ought to will as a result of the representation of the ought or of its determining vocation. This ought is supposed to hover before it in consciousness as the ground of [its] act of will.* |

In order to make this point clear by means of its antithesis, [first] posit that the I does not determine itself as a result of the *ought*. Two cases {then become possible}: {either [the I]} *does not* {determine itself} *at all*, which it *could* do—thus remaining in the state of contemplation—or [the I] in fact wills, only not as a result of the [representation of the] ought. {Then} two further cases {become possible}: either {[the I] determines itself} according to the given concept or not. The latter once again {makes} two cases {possible}: either [the I determines itself] according to no *concept*, or according to a *different one*. It is not possible [that the I determine itself] according to no [concept]; freedom, self-determination, or willing just are the transition from ideality to reality. | Thus [it must determine itself] according to a different [concept]. In that case, we would have to ascribe to the I (which in our view is merely the exhibition of a determinate concept) an ability to absolutely create a concept for itself, to make something up for itself in thought [*sich etwas auszudenken*]. Whether there may be such an I is not our concern. The I that we have deduced and about which we are talking is not [such an I].—Thus {[the I] could determine itself} according to this [concept]

---

6. [Fichte's marginal note:] Concept of a *motive*; a concept that is known immediately as the ground of an actual willing; there the [concept] of the ought or of determination is a concept of *that which wills* (StA 297).

7. GA has Lecture 8 beginning after this parenthetical remark; StA is not clear on the break between Lecture 7 and Lecture 8. See comments in n. 1 in this lecture.

and not as a result of [the representation of the] *ought*; [the latter] {would} not {be present} as a motive of the will in consciousness; [the representation of the ought] {would} not be linked [with the will] as a ground. [The I] would therefore have to possess some other motive. This {could be} either pleasure in the content *of the concept* ({this case} is posited deliberately here), in which case the I would not be the *pure* instrument of the concept. This is impossible. This is certainly possible in general, since there is in this instance a transition from a concept to [its] realization, even though it cannot be conceived how this realization could become a motive for freedom. Even granting this, the concept would not in this case be a ground; rather, the I and its absolute freedom would be a ground for what is established (necessarily, since there is no other concept in this instance).[8] But [the I] would have to be able to become the ground of every other antithetical concept. The concept or its content is actualized materially, but it is not *through itself a ground* simply by virtue of its form. The [problem] that has been formulated has not been resolved. This {is} therefore the summit of the analysis. If this consciousness is moral, this is its absolute essence.

Theorem [*Satz*]: every act of will must have a motive. Proof: willing is a transition of the *I* from the ideality to reality. [The I] must therefore have an image of itself that is supposed to be realized through this transition.

Expressed in a different way: the ideality that the I itself possesses as its object is a determination of the I and thus a characteristic feature of it; [this ideality] must transition into reality through willing. {This theorem,} augmented, purified, and refined, is never properly clarified in the theory of the will [{*Dieser Satz*} *Vermehrt, reinigt, u. läutert gar sehr die auch nirgends recht ins reine gebrachte Willenslehre*]. The content of the concept is not a motive, for it is foreign to the I and does not say anything about it [*redet nicht von ihm*]. The ought, however, [is a motive], for it does say something about [the I] [*denn dies redet von ihm*].

---

8. Halle has Lecture 8 beginning at this point; see n. 1 in this lecture.

The claim [*Satz*] is thus that the ought, which the concept carries with itself absolutely without any assistance from the will or freedom, must be the motive of the will, otherwise the concept as ground has not entered into consciousness.

The analysis is complete; we have arrived at the very transition where the concept immediately passes over into the domain of objectivity.[9] |

---

9. CAUER: Our *I*, as the absolute instrument of the concept and of its life, has no other possible concept that it could realize (here [we have] abstracted away completely from the empirical I). Thus it cannot will anything else besides the content of the *ought*. But the I could just as well will only *for the sake of its freedom*. Just like the ought, freedom is an image that the I has of itself, and it can also be actualized. In this instance, the concept would not be *a ground*, but rather the I would be something completely self-sufficient. The concept of a motive must be explained at this point. [A motive] is a concept that is recognized immediately as a ground of the will, as in the other case the ought [is so recognized]. We have tacitly assumed the higher claim that every act of will must have a motive, for willing is a transition from something ideal to something real. The I must hover before itself in an image that is supposed to be realized. It is precisely this image that is called the motive of willing. The content in the I = X is therefore not a motive, but rather the *ought* [is a motive], for this speaks about the I itself. The claim can be expressed in this way: the ought must occur as a motive of the will, otherwise the causality of the concept has not entered into consciousness at all. The concept carries the ought immediately along with itself. The assigned analysis of the concept—which is a ground—is now actually completed. We have arrived at the point where the concept actually enters objectivity as a motive.

Lecture 8

(July 10, 1812)

II/13, 327

Consequences and additional comments: The I *ought* [to do something]; its essence is this ought, and nothing more. [The I] is nothing other than the life of the concept. Hence | [the I] is exhaustively determined through the very same concept through which it is also created. [The concept] {is thus} the author [*Urheber*] and creator of the I in the full sense.

Furthermore, a *world*, [which is] an object of an objective intuition, is supposed to come into being through the freedom of the I. Only then is the I the principle of the world, and according to the present view there is no other {world} besides the one that the I creates.[1] (Here we are not concerned about the faint trace of a different view from another context; however, we could assure ourselves that it is correct from the higher standpoint of our science.) Yet, the I ought to create [a world] according to the concept (perhaps it can only create [in this way]). The entire content of the world is therefore posited and prescribed within the concept. The I is free with respect to willing and therefore [with respect to] acting efficaciously and being a principle. A world is not necessarily posited by [the I]. But the I is supposed to will and act efficaciously according to the concept, and this brings forth a world. Thus, according to its formal being, the world is simply posited through the

---

1. CAUER: Now, in addition, a *world* is supposed to come into being through this I; in the series of our deduction there is indeed no world other than that which is created by the I.

concept and ought to exist, just as it is a result of [the concept] and is determined through it alone.

The world, or at least the true world, which is the only one we are talking about here (we are not concerned with the illusory world [*Scheinwelt*] here) is the effect and precipitate [*Absaz*] of the concept into objective appearance. [The world] itself is, in the form of objective intuition, just what the concept is in its pure form as an image. These two, which are in themselves absolutely one, are only distinct by means of these two forms, and the I is the point of synthetic unity for both.[2]

Before we set out in a complete way the perspective regarding the world as such and morality that follows from this, | {we want} to definitively exclude an error that we have already [noted].

Freedom is really the absolute transition point from what is purely an image into an objective form *within* consciousness. The objective form is absolute, for in its sphere it is an image of the absolute; it is its own point of origin and principle. But with respect to its content [the objective form] is not supposed to be its own principle, but rather it is supposed to be what results from the pure form as its principle. This contradiction is mediated in consciousness through freedom.

As the ground of free determination and thereby of the world, the concept that is being assumed takes on the form of the *ought*, or of a law for freedom, within this synthetic relation. {The concept} is not described by [the ought or the law of freedom] in its purity, rather it is described this way only in relation to something different that is external to it. There is no ought or lawfulness within it but rather only in this relation.

---

2. CAUER: Yet, the I is free with respect to willing or not willing. Thus, no world is posited through the I—it is indifferent with respect to a world. Considered under the rule of the concept, however, the I ought to will and act efficaciously. Thus the world is posited immediately in a formal way as regards its existence by the concept. Through the medium of the I the true world is the effect and self-precipitate of the concept into objective appearance. The very same content belongs in both the concept and the world; only the world is in *objective intuition* the very same thing that the concept is in a purely intelligible form. Thus only the form comprises the distinction.

Thus, there is an external [and] uncontestable criterion for grasping this concept in case one is somehow not already familiar with it, as well as for distinguishing it from other concepts, just in case there are any. It is said that it proclaims itself as something that ought to be; I *ought* [to do something]; the world ought to be this way. Absolute postulate | of an act of will and of an order of the world. Hence, whatever concept lacks this characteristic is certainly not the one we are discussing.

However, this *ought* is merely something contingent, an external feature produced by way of determination through an association rather than the inner essence [of the concept] itself. It is indeed just a criterion or an *image*. Hence, someone who only knows how to describe | the moral concept as a moral law, a categorical imperative, a postulate, is only familiar with it in an image or proxy. The whole theory of ethics that is constructed on the basis of this concept is not itself [the theory of ethics] but rather only an image of it, albeit one that is quite useful in life. [Such a theory] in no way fulfills scientific requirements. [To do so,] one must recognize that the concept is absolutely *determined through itself* (*through itself* in the pure, self-enclosed theory of ethics; in the *Wissenschaftslehre* or theory of God [it is determined through] the inner essence of God).[3]

I said at the outset that one needs to derive this *ought*, as has just now taken place. [The ought] acquires its true meaning within the derivation. [The ought] is not to be simply assumed. A personal observation {in addition to this}. It is clear that I have in mind the Kantian view, which,

---

3. HALLE: Freedom as transition steps into the middle here; in this relationship the concept assumes the form of an ought, as a *law of freedom*. In this way, the higher enters into the lower, while freedom retains its value. The concept only enters consciousness in this connection, as the law of freedom, on account of the linkage. The ought is not the concept itself but rather merely expresses this relationship. This CATEGORICAL NATURE [CATEGORICITÄT] is merely a CRITERION = an external image of the true concept. Whoever classifies the concept as a postulate [*den Begriff aufstellt im Postulat*] is only familiar with its reflection in the composite of the I; such a theory of ethics can only be an image of the theory of ethics. It would suffice for practical life but not as an element of philosophy, not as a science. One must know that the concept is determined through itself (IV/6, 97–98).

though criticized as unscientific, is nevertheless flawless in a practical sense and is worthy of honor considering the wretched age in which it was first articulated. What then does the view of the *Wissenschaftslehre* have over it? In what way have I accomplished something before your eyes that allows me to criticize [the Kantian view]? Through the mere analysis of the proposition *the concept is a ground*. Was this proposition still hidden from Kant? No, on the contrary, the clear knowledge of and engagement with it is the chief reason for why Kant's theory of ethics achieved so much (and for the improvement of the species it has achieved infinitely much). But how does [Kant] understand [this proposition]? Within an I. That is the tacit assumption. He already possesses consciousness as something that is familiar. | Hence, [his theory is founded on] mere facticity.[4] We do not {proceed} this way; {we} allow the *I* and consciousness to first come into being, hence the completely different result. Why [do we proceed in this way]? For your instruction. |

---

4. Fichte is very likely thinking here of Kant's famous discussion of the "fact of reason" in the *Critique of Practical Reason* (AA 5:31–33).

Lecture 9

(July 14, 1812)

View of the world, and of morality, from this point of view.

(1) The only thing that absolutely exists is the *concept*, a purely spiritual [*geistig*] being. Many cannot even elevate themselves to a notion of this being. For them, the concept is merely the expression of an objective knowing, a likeness or copy of a thing. Here it depends on each person's organ. Pure thinking [versus] objective thinking. {What can be done} for someone who does not possess [the organ for] the former [kind of thinking]? Whoever possesses it thereby *knows it*. One can only know it through such an immediate knowing; once again, philosophy is itself only the image of such a knowing.

Defined via antithesis, {one could only say that this pure spiritual being is} *not* objective; {not} in this duality but rather in its purity and unity. That duality is the characteristic {of all products of objective thought}, namely, that a being {is} the result of a knowing or *vice versa*. This {is} completely denied in this case. {Rather, what is being proposed} is a knowing that bears the characteristic of reality within itself. In itself [it is] true, clear, certain, and real. The immaterial, pure intelligibility, or the spiritual world as such exists in itself and through itself. Idea or something that is simply seen [*bloßes Gesicht*].[1]

This claim, which others put forward in a figurative way, is asserted here with complete, literal seriousness, just as the words sound. Others, even when it is taken in the best way, {comprehend [the spiritual world]} in a reciprocal relation with materiality [*Jene, wo es etwa am besten noch genommen wird [fassen es] in einer Wechselbeziehung mit der Materialität*]. We [on the other hand] grasp it in and through itself alone. They talk about a spiritual world, {but} they shudder if this pronouncement is taken seriously and *only* a spiritual world {is spoken of}.

Objective world, nature—{there is} no such thing {for us}; it is completely denied. For them {on the other hand} [the objective world or nature] is what is absolutely true. Schelling pitied me for having no nature. I respond in the same way.[2]

{In fact}, it is he who has no *nature*, only blind chance. {One must} relinquish one or the other, either spirit or nature. They will never be united. Their unification is partly pretense and lie, partly an unintended inconsistency [brought about] by inner feeling.

Truly actual being is spiritual; there is no other being.

({This is how the matter is regarded} *in the theory of ethics*, which, just in case it exists, is given through a higher organ and develops along with it. Just as feeling posits the world that can be felt, and not the realm of light, which only exists for the eye, so sensible intuition [*sinnliche Ansicht*] does not {posit} the spiritual realm. Only the spiritual eye does so.

---

1. CAUER: This concept is not objective; there is no talk here of a duality of being and image. Such knowing is completely denied here—our concept is in itself real and subsists on its own. We thus have in mind something totally immaterial, something purely *intelligible* that exists in light and is itself only light. According to our point of view, this spirit [*Geist*] is the world, the only world that there is. An objective world = nature is *completely* denied. This is how things stand in the theory of ethics, which brings with itself a higher organ for looking into an intelligible world. The fact that this intelligible world is once again an image of a higher, absolute being is still hidden at this point.

2. HALLE: Schelling once lamented the fact that I knew nothing of nature, but I pity him even more for the fact that he knows nothing of spirit (IV/6, 98).

Now, the fact that, when this [spiritual world] is considered as it appears in itself, the new insight arises that it is [itself in turn] only the image of a higher, absolutely [. . .]³ and incomprehensible being does not belong here. We should keep it to ourselves lest we adopt a point of view beyond the theory of ethics.)

(2) This spiritual being is not dead, as is self-evident, otherwise it would be entirely nonexistent. Rather it becomes dead through our picturing it and attending to it, forgetting that this is our life in attending to it. It is alive (as may be shown, among other places, even in our attending to it). It is a life that permeates the *being that is posited by us as a concept in the form of the concept*, the vitality of that concept and being, to which two things belong [*Es ist ein durch* jenes, von uns als Begriff in der Form des Begriffes abgesetze Wesen *durchdrungnes Leben: jenes Begriffs u. Wesens Lebendigkeit, worin da liegt zweierlei*]:

(a) This concept is a dynamic, self-expressing life; it can exhibit itself and set itself down in a product that carries its stamp in itself.

(b) It possesses a living reflection of itself and is conscious of itself as *this* concept, as life and power, as precipitating this or that in case it deposits anything, and therefore {is conscious} of this product itself. I said that {*it is conscious of*} *itself as a life*, and this fact is to be particularly emphasized; [it is conscious of itself] {as precipitating something} by itself, thus as {a} *free* {life}. All consciousness of its efficacy is necessarily associated with this consciousness of its freedom. It is therefore free either to act efficaciously and to express itself in consciousness or not.⁴, ⁵ |

---

3. The editors of StA indicate that several illegible words appear at this point.

4. [Fichte's marginal note:] Consciousness of freedom [is the] condition of the consciousness of a causality, of its product. But freedom {is} something absolute that can either exist or not.

5. CAUER: It is in itself living—it is conscious of itself as a life and a free power and as depositing itself in a product. Thus it brings with itself a reflection of its life. It is conscious of itself as a life, and thus it is also conscious of itself as *free* with respect to externalization. Freedom only occurs in consciousness—it actually does not *truly* exist but is merely a form of life.

These possible *expressions*, as attaching themselves to the immediate consciousness of the life of the concept or of the I, and further determining it from out of its mere possibility, are not objects of an *objective consciousness*. A being arises that exists because it is seen, for it only exists because freedom, which is absolutely visible and is accompanied in all of its expressions by seeing, determines itself to this, | ({because} [freedom] is the absolute ground of this being that could just as well not exist).[6]

A truly objective world exists only through the life of the concept, otherwise not at all. There is no other {world} besides [the world] of the products of freedom. {Thus we have} *being and its image*, the objective world. This is how the relationship goes. Where the vulgar point of view sees an image, we see being; where there is being [for the vulgar point of view], we see merely an image.

(3) This is how it is, and with that this point of view is complete [*ist diese Ansicht geschlossen*]. There is no more room for an objective world that is not a product of freedom. If this point of view is true and exhaustive, it follows immediately that if [an objective world that is not a product of freedom] has pretensions to existence, it does not truly exist at all but rather [only exists] in appearance—the *appearance* of the true world to which belong the two basic elements that have been set forth [earlier]. The sheer visibility [of freedom] must contribute this. How the two are related is left aside for a different inquiry. The view that we have set forth must decide whether or not it is able to demonstrate the nullity of the other world; it may [simply] insist upon its insight into its nonexistence. The world disappears and vanishes into nothing. I will set forth in a note a point of

---

6. HALLE: In truth, it expresses itself within consciousness, in the reflection of this life, it makes an image for itself [*bildet sich*] of this life as an I, as a form. And thus a free life. The expression as something possible simply occurs in a factual way in consciousness (IV/6, 99).

Lecture 9

StA 308

view that is entirely identical with this one and that exists factually.[7] |

Conclusion. Through this point of view what one has previously called a theory of ethics is transformed into a *theory of being* (theory of true being, of genuine reality). The difference is that a theory of ethics assumes freedom as a possibility of being or not being, hence as an element that unites both, as an immediately known, true reality, and subsumes it under laws. For [the theory of ethics] this freedom is the truly primary and original being. (That such a theory cannot henceforth be asserted is clear, for where is the element of lawfulness that is completely different from freedom and opposed to it supposed to come from?) The theory that we set forth here does not assume freedom but rather derives it as a mere *form of appearance*. [It derives freedom] not as something that belongs immediately within being but rather only within the *visibility of being*; it is a synthetic member of a relation, namely, the relation between

II/13, 332

what in fact does not exist (the expression of life | in an image) and that which alone exists in an absolute way (the life of the concept itself).[8]

If one calls the assertion of a merely illusory life physics, {then one can call the theory of true life} metaphysics. This would be the first point.

---

7. HALLE: This is what the view of the world looks like from this standpoint, and with that it is complete. There is no room for an objective world that is not a product of freedom. [. . .] It must be that the true world thus described has somehow reflected itself in a different way or cast a reflection of itself; this other world must be only a product of the *visibility* of the true world. This world cannot be explained on the basis of the principle of morality; our current point of view can only insist upon its nullity (IV/6, 99–100).

8. CAUER: *Result of what has been said:* The *theory of ethics* is thus transformed into a *theory of being*—the difference is that a theory of ethics assumes freedom as a fact—not freedom in the sense of the ABSOLUTENESS of what is absolutely primary but rather as the possibility of a duality: of being and not being. It subsumes this freedom under laws. In this way the primary and absolute being of the theory of ethics is actually not a being but rather a mere potentiality for being or not being.

Lecture 10

(July 15, 1812)

However, if one wants to retain the words "moral," "theory of ethics," etc., in order to first link this discourse to the vulgar point of view, as well as {for} the pragmatic end of human education [*Menschenbildung*], how does the meaning of these expressions thereby change?

First of all, it is clear that one must occupy the standpoint of the connection or relation of true being to the [being of] an image, since the concept of | morality posits freedom in the sense indicated, i.e., indifference with respect to willing, and so first [posits] a willing as such. One must therefore assume an I that is self-sufficient and indifferent in relation to its determination prior to its being determined through the concept. This {is} the absolute presupposition for a theory of ethics in the genuine sense. The theory of ethics therefore does not occupy the standpoint of truth but rather that of appearance ({and,} in case it is supposed to actually be scientific, it must do so with the intention of dissolving appearance into truth and annihilating it).[1]

Two questions can be raised about this I relative to morality: one in respect to *being* and the other in respect to *becoming*.

---

1. HALLE: A theory of ethics does not occupy the standpoint of truth universally but rather that of appearance. Not in order to create an illusion; rather in order to dissolve appearance and lead it back to the truth and annihilate illusion in truth. A theory of ethics is φαινομενολογια (IV/6, 100–101).

(1) Under what condition does the I actually and truly exist? And, since the I necessarily appears to itself, and nothing else new is expressed through the form of the I besides self-appearance, how must it appear to itself if it truly and really exists? The *theory of appearance* of the I {answers this question}. I say theory of appearance and nothing more; it is in no way a genuinely practical theory of [how the I] *constitutes* itself, for this would presuppose a genuine freedom, which does not exist. If the I exists, then it necessarily appears in such-and-such a way to itself in consciousness, for consciousness is the reflection of actual being. Hence, you who raise this question should look within yourselves. If you appear then {you exist}, [otherwise] you do not in fact exist. The I, that which appears, does not create being, but rather being creates the appearance of the I. The actual {I} is only for itself in its appearance, not immediately in its being. It can only infer the latter from the former. Thus: how do I exist? | The question answers itself, if you pose it to yourself. [You exist] as you appear to yourself. Am I actual? Then you must appear to yourself in such and such a way. The system of this appearance {is} the theory of ethics.²

{Being creates | the appearance} of the true I; it is therefore assumed as the connecting point for the antithetical proposition that the I could also *not appear* this way to itself and yet {could still} appear to itself. In that case, however, the latter would not be the true I but rather an empty, null image of the same. *Immorality* is therefore truly a sheer nothing in this theory.

This theory of appearance is supposed to be the system that we set forth, and so it is. The question that we posed {about the appearance of the I} has already been completely answered by what has been said. The I is the life of the absolute concept. The true I must therefore appear to itself completely as such and as *nothing else* than the exhibited concept that objectifies itself in an existence. *The Word*

---

2. HALLE: Thus, whoever wants to know whether his I is the appearance of the true I or not looks into himself—if he appears to himself as the theory of ethics exhibits it, then it is so; otherwise such an I does not exist (IV/6, 101).

StA 311

II/13, 334

became flesh.³ An I in whose consciousness some principle other than the absolute concept were to occur would to that extent not be a true [I] but rather a merely illusory I [*ScheinIch*]. That such a different principle could occur in consciousness is in any event posited through the visibility of the pure life by means of antithesis. {The I must appear to itself} *entirely and absolutely as nothing other than the life of the absolute concept*. [This] is the encompassing and absolutely exhaustive formulation for the entire theory of ethics. {In this way it attains} the highest simplicity.⁴

{An} absolute concept that is determined simply through itself is {called} *reason*. *Among other things*, it is said that reason is practical. It is better {to say} that [reason] alone is practical, and only that which is absolutely practical is reason, {for reason is} the absolute image. All other [images] are images of the form of the absolute image; thus they carry

---

3. [Fichte's marginal note:] {The rule is recommended} merely practically, for the formation of the character. In case one does not understand: simply deny the sensible world and cling only to the higher [world] (Christianity {also recognizes this}), to the pure concept as the image of God. Religious ethics. To be the instrument [of the pure concept]. In [the Gospel of] John. The whole doctrine of Jesus's being in God and of the being of {Jesus's} disciple in Jesus. *Death* leads one to become alive [*Belebung*]. Renunciation of the world, dying away to the world, etc. Without this recognition, Christianity in its entirety has no meaning. The rest is completely [StA 311] harmless, practically speaking. In God's will, one always once again occupies the place in the sensible world that one is supposed to have.

4. CAUER: The true and the real exists *for itself* only in its appearance, not in its *being*; being can only be inferred from appearance. The theory of ethics provides the criterion for the actual existence of the truly real I. This must be distinguished from an unreal, null I. Immorality, vice, [or] sin are, according to this theory, simply nothingness [*Nichtigkeit*] itself on display. Only morality is actual and true. The theory of ethics that is supposed to be presented should in fact be such a phenomenology. The I is the life of the absolute concept—thus the true I must appear to itself as the objectifying concept that exhibits itself in an existence. Put otherwise: the true I must be the Word = concept that has become flesh. Any other I in which something other than the absolute concept occurs would thus not be the true I but rather a mere illusion of the same. That something else could occur in the self-consciousness of the I is posited via *antithesis*. There must therefore be an answer [to the question] about how the I would have to appear to itself just in case it were true. One could also call this absolute concept reason. Then one would understand what it means [to say that] reason is *practical*.

with themselves particular characteristics that are created through a relation, as we have clearly seen in the case of the concept of freedom. For this reason, they are concepts of a concept. [They are] seen by means of a characteristic, hence [they are] *understood. Understanding.* Understanding is never immediately practical.[5]

This formula is clear. One could desire an external criterion for the absolute concept. {Something} external. Hence, the assumption is that there would be still other concepts outside of the absolute [concept] in relation to which and in opposition with which it would express its absoluteness.

The primary and most original criterion is obvious; the next concept is of an objective | world, an externalization of freedom. The concept would have to express itself as absolute in relation to this [concept], i.e., as absolutely creative of objectivity, {as} something new that creates in an unprecedented way.[6] The opposite would be objects that are supposed to exist for the sake of something else, as means to an end. The former is not at all [a means to an end]. Hence the formula: absolutely creative, for its own sake, an end in itself [*SelbstZwek*], not a means for a different end. From the point of view set out here, these [formulae] are entirely correct. The I must appear as creating in an absolute way that which is an end in itself, that which simply ought to be, that which has no purpose outside of itself; only in this way is [the I] the life of the absolute concept.[7]

A second external criterion for the absolute concept has already been discussed at length. Because the life of the

---

5. CAUER: The other concepts are therefore concepts of the understanding. But understanding is always *theoretical*, just as reason alone is *practical*.

6. CAUER: The concept must be absolutely creative—initiating a new life that has never before been seen [*nie dagewesen ist*], creative for its own sake.

7. [Fichte's marginal note:] A paradigm of the actual world. [The actual world] appears in the idea before it exists in objective intuition. Plato—who in this respect puts modern *Naturphilosophen* to shame. There is the as yet not well understood question of whether the distinction between the world that is supposed to be created practically and that of mere appearance had become properly clear to him. It can be said so of the latter only in a very derivative sense.

concept appears as a formal life through itself, as a *potentiality*, and thus as free to will or not, the concept appears as a postulate of the will, as a formal law, or as an ought. It is obvious that this must be the view of the concept that is most proper to the theory of ethics to the extent that it assumes freedom and subsumes it under a law. It has been shown that this point of view is not the truth | but rather is merely appearance. The concept, if it in fact appears, is not capable of either living and acting efficaciously or not. | Rather, it does act efficaciously, and it has merely exhibited itself in an *image* of its efficacious action as if it could have also not [acted efficaciously], in order to produce an image [*bilden*] of its absolute life. It has also been shown, and is once again made evident through what has been said, that this appearance of the ought is completely inseparable from the will in the context of appearance, and that the ought must necessarily appear as a motive of willing, i.e., as the ideal of the I that immediately spills over into objective reality. This criterion is therefore infallible. The concept occurs in consciousness necessarily with the characteristic of an ought, and no other [concept] can occur with this characteristic.

Lecture 11

(July 16, 1812)

That which is revealed to the I as what it absolutely ought to do is called its duty. A *theory of duty* [*PflichtenLehre*] is thus subsumed under the theory of ethics. I say that it is *subsumed* because this concept [of duty] expresses only the what, the quality. A will that willed it would be a dutiful [will]. It would not yet be *moral* by virtue of this alone, since it is part [of being moral] that the I would act in this way for duty's sake and for the sake of the ought, {that} this would be the will's motive, as has been shown already.[1]

Another formula {is made apparent in this way}: the I must appear as willing its duty simply for the sake of duty; duty, with the characteristic that it ought to be willed by the I absolutely, is the absolute concept. Only if [the I] wills [the concept] for this reason is [the I] the life of the absolute concept.

I have added that [duty] is revealed absolutely as duty. This duty is the absolute concept itself, which is only absolute insofar as it is not derived from anything else. It exhibits itself within consciousness as being underived from anything else, as has already been clarified under the first criterion. Even though this is obvious, it is worthwhile to recall here, given some prevalent errors, that no one can devise his duty for himself or infer it, that there is, therefore,

StA 314

---

1. HALLE: According to us the theory of ethics must contain *in itself* the theory of duty, [though it will] not itself be a theory of duty. It is part of morality that duty is done for duty's sake; without intuiting itself as the instrument of the concept, a will would be merely dutiful (IV/6, 103).

no theory of duty *a priori*, and it cannot be the goal of our theory of ethics to establish such a theory.² (Unfortunately, this is how things seem in *some theories of ethics*.) Each person is referred to his own consciousness in this regard.³

Is there anything left that is yet to be established by our theory of ethics, which is without doubt an *a priori* science, once it has completed the analysis of the proposition set forth [at the beginning of the lecture]? (I want to introduce an answer to this question by way of what was said at the beginning.)⁴

Answer. The criteria for the absoluteness of the concept are at the same time the criteria for the requisite appearance of the I, and this is how we have considered them. {We are now looking for} criteria that belong to a higher level and that can be known factually. Thus, someone who does not distinguish | the absolute concept and therefore {has not grasped} its appearance can indeed {recognize} on the basis of the [originally assumed] proposition whether it is the {appearance} of the absolute life; likewise {in answering the question of} whether he wills that something absolutely ought to be or wills his duty for duty's sake. In this manner the phenomenon has still other criteria. {We want to} present these completely and in this way to present a complete image of the phenomenon of the true I as far as possible here below in the physical world. {A} *complete theory of appearance* [*Erscheinungslehre*].

This {can be exhibited} *a priori* because it presents the mere form and abstracts away from all content. It may be part of this that we know the phenomenology of an I as such in a complete way, in order to distinguish what | can be inferred about the true I on account of its form from what can be inferred about the merely apparent [*schein-*

---

2. CAUER: Therefore, there cannot be a theory of duty *a priori*, since duties cannot be derived as consequences. Each person is therefore referred to his own consciousness.

3. HALLE: If, in some systems, duties are derived as consequences, then that is a tremendous misunderstanding. Each person is referred to his own consciousness regarding duty (IV/6, 103).

4. CAUER: There is no material theory of duty.

bare] I. It is quite obvious that, should we want to present such a phenomenology of the I with complete precision, we would [likewise] have to present the whole of philosophy, at least from the perspective of an absolute concept. This cannot be what we aim at here since we want to treat the theory of ethics as a particular science. Therefore we must, as it were, apply propositions from other sciences like theorems. A stable principle for this kind of treatment quickly becomes apparent: {our task is to present} a theory of appearance of the true and real I; a theory of the I, hence, a phenomenology that, since previously we were dealing with a theory of being, is nevertheless an absolute phenomenology, not simply a phenomenon of a phenomenon as is physics.

(2) {The theory of ethics is thus [one] in search of} a different perspective [from that of being] in the sense of *becoming*. How does the merely illusory I become the true [I]? Furthermore, if the investigation is supposed to be useful, how can [the merely illusory I] *make itself* into [the true I]? [Answers to these questions would comprise] a genuinely practical and pragmatic *theory of the art* [*Kunstlehre*] of morality. The assumption could be, first of all, that some given immoral I is supposed to transform itself into a moral [I], and that it would like to have such an art. With respect to this the following point should be considered, namely, that this desire or the application of this art already presupposes the will to be moral. But this is itself already morality; it is the good or righteous will. Hence, what is in any event already obvious and quite well known also becomes apparent here, namely, that no one can make himself moral but must instead come to be moral, plain and simple. [Furthermore,] this rebirth is just as little a work of freedom as is the first [natural] birth. A theory could therefore | only want to teach the art of empowering and fortifying a good will that is already present against faltering or fluctuating. [This art] could be correctly called asceticism [*Ascetik*]. It is not our intention to present this here, to the extent that I we are dealing with something higher. Still, it is clear that the basic principles of such asceticism must be discovered on the basis of our theory.

Second, the assumption could be that the great universal I, the entire human species, ought to elevate itself to the *morality* of the whole through a reflective art [*besonnene Kunst*]. Therefore such an art should be demanded, and it might be called the theory of the education of the human species [*Erziehungslehre des Menschengeschlechts*], pedagogy in the highest and most universal sense. Subordinate to it would be pedagogy in the narrower sense, the theory of the education of children, the theory of law-giving, the theory of moral formation [*sittlichen Bildung*] through the church, etc. We will not present this extensive theory, which requires multiple principles.

However, we will, without deliberately intending to do so, frequently come into contact with these principles in merely carrying out our plan.

(To linger for a moment on this issue: it is clear that this reflective and artful education of the species must proceed on the basis of particular individuals. Now for the first time talk of such an art can arise. Up till now, the human species was educated by God; indeed, {it will} continue to be educated this way for yet a long time, until [this art] awakens within the species and it undertakes its own education with freedom and unerring skill. One should not regard this as presumption nor think that humanity will be worse off in that case. God educates humanity only up to the point from which it acquires the capacity | to educate itself, and that is his genuine intention. When humanity is self-sufficient, God will not be educating it any less; it is only that [he will] no longer [do so] in an immediate way, in the form of the blind development of nature, but rather [God will do so] in the form of clear and reflective concepts. Human beings are never anything but God's instruments; the only difference is whether they are [God's instruments] as moral [beings] who possess their own clear consciousness or lack [this clear consciousness] and so are not genuinely [God's instruments]. It is furthermore obvious that such a reflective education would not exist until, at the very least, the goal of morality is clearly and distinctly recognized, so that it could become a force in the world. As for what has been accomplished up till now with human beings by their

II/13, 338   educator and leader, one can conclude without unkindness that a clear knowledge of the goal and an efficacious will for it were not the driving forces.)[5, 6] |

---

5. CAUER: It is clear that this universal theory [of education] must proceed on the basis of individuals—indeed, what is being discussed is a reflective art. It is only *now* that such an art can really be discussed for the first time; it is obvious that humanity has been educated up to this point, though by God, and it will be educated by God for a long time until it is in a state to educate itself, and then God will educate [it] properly for the first time. The difference is only whether he educates in the form of a blind force of nature or in the form of clear reflective concepts. [Humanity] should and must reach that point. For that to happen, at the very least the goal = that of *pure morality*—must first be known and it must be known in such a way that it becomes a *physical force* in humanity.

6. HALLE: Such an art can be spoken of for the first time in our age. Until now the human species was, of course, educated by God and will continue to be so educated until it can educate itself. This is not presumptuousness, for God educates humanity until [it has] the capacity to educate itself. Even then, God will not have ceased to educate. Only then does God properly educate for the first time (IV/6, 103).

Lecture 12

(July 17, 1812)

Historical application. My {conception of the theory of ethics as} a *theory of being*. As pure *theory* [*Theorie*]. {Such a conception can be found already} in *Plato*: things {are} reflections of ideas, things that are seen [*Gesichte*]—the antithesis [between] *objective* and *pure* {knowing} is quite clear. It is not clear whether [Plato] made the distinction between two objective forms of the world, as being [on the one hand] a *product* of freedom, and as being [on the other hand] the absolutely given, empirical [form of the world] lacking any relation to freedom. Regarding the former, [Plato's view] is entirely correct, that is, provided it is only asserted in this regard. Regarding the latter [it is correct] in a very limited and mediated sense, as least {in the sense} that the whole, not the particular, is the result of an idea [*Gesichte*].

StA 318 | Still, this does not belong here. {This would be the view} of the *Platonist*; I think there may be more [who hold it].[1, 2]

---

1. CAUER: Is it not the case that the point of view we have presented already prevailed at an earlier time? By all means. The view that currently prevails belongs only to a small piece of time. (1) *Theoretically.* Plato already presented the idea as what is primary and defined things as copies of it. It is admittedly not clear as to whether he made the distinction between a true objective world (= a product of freedom) and a merely illusory world (absolutely given). (2) *Practically*—for the cultivation [*Bildung*] of the character. This point of view is based on a character that is seized by the pure causality of the concept. One such [practical] teaching is Christianity. John's Gospel and his other writings should be considered as the foundation. There it is said directly that the entire sensible world is nothing; the concept is continually regarded in its original meaning as the image of God, the will of God. Only to the degree that a human being attains this image does he *exist* at all. Christ is presented as a pure likeness [*Abbild*] [of this image of God].

2. HALLE: (1) One might wonder whether some of this point of view has been seen previously. Obviously, it is quite an ancient manner of thinking. This is [true] first of

{Let us consider} the difference between the standpoint of truth and that of appearance. {This} is of infinite importance, inasmuch as it is here that the confused inquiries into and questions about freedom are brought to an end. (Here it is often love and inclination that cause the confusion. Proper love does not cause one to be confused; rather, it is always the old love of the I [*IchLiebe*], which decks itself out in a delightful way, [that causes the confusion]. This is not in itself my concern, nor is it advisable to take you on this detour, for I have the utmost confidence in all of you.)

{Regarding the standpoint} of truth: the absolute concept has life, power, causality, and is through itself the creator of appearance. [It is first of all the creator] of the I, and then of the appearance of the act of will, the action, and the intuition of this I. Every appearance of this concept must actually and in fact appear; the *actual appearance* {must} be the same as that which is possible on the basis of the concept. In this case the appearance is moral, in the sense that this term is supposed to possess. An individual I (and there is no other [I] in actual appearance) must appear as a certain limited, regular determination [*Regel*] of the

---

all theoretically, [second of all] practically. Can a theoretical doctrine be discovered that posits the concept as primary and the objective as the image of the concept? Plato has just such a [doctrine]. He teaches that things are reflections of ideas. [An] idea is a pure image; things [are] copies. (We do not agree with his [doctrine of] ideas in God.) [. . .] Next, only practically—for the cultivation of the character. The one for whom the connection of the world does not matter but who is concerned only about inner purity knows that nothing but the concept is the ground of the world. The sensible world is nothing to him, albeit he has no explanation of it. [Cultivation] proceeds from the character that is seized by the causality of the concept. According to Christian teaching, the world is denied. The foundation of Christianity is John's Gospel and, as a reflection of it, [John's] epistles. Christianity cannot explain the appearance of the sensible world. It is not concerned with it but says that it is nothing. Christianity regards the concept in its original meaning as the image and will of God. This is the only thing that exists, and the human being exists to the extent that his life is the life of the concept, otherwise he does not exist. JESUS is presented as the reflection of the divine image. It is further said that everyone else who wants to live must dwell in this likeness of the divine life, i.e., in Jesus. There is a leap [*Uebersprung*] here. Everyone can immediately be like Jesus and does not need to be in Jesus. That may perhaps be conceded. On the other hand, it is clear in John that others do not exist, that they are lying in the grave (IV/6, 105–106).

absolute concept. The I is moral just in case the actuality of appearance, within these limits, appears to be equivalent to what is possible for the concept without any discontinuity or alteration. The concept lives and appears.

{Regarding the standpoint} of appearance: Here the I, the image of the concept, is supposed to have power and life, to be a principle. A theory founded on this standpoint can only be either a theory of appearance (if it knows that it is talking about appearance | and acknowledges the truth in the background), or a *theory of illusion* [*ScheinLehre*] (if it does not recognize [the truth] and takes the appearance to be the thing [itself]). In that case illusion, error, and deception arise in its judgments.

Theory of appearance: The I is the absolutely faithful, true image of the life of the concept, and the concept alone is visible within it. As is the I that you see, and that you alone see, | so is the concept that you do not see, within the limits that characterize this I within appearance in general. For example, if you want to know {whether the concept appears, then look at how [the I] appears to you}. You cannot see the concept; look at yourself.

Theory of illusion: {a theory} that believes in an actual power of the I, defines it, and wants to prescribe rules for its determination. (In which instance is the theory of ethics supposed to be pragmatic? In which instance should it be something different, pure theory? What is [the theory of ethics] in the shape of a theory of appearance?).

{But this is} completely false. The concept of freedom obtains in two cases, either when the I in fact wills as it ought, or when the I does not will. In the first case {the theory of illusion wants to say} that I also could have not willed. But if you actually and in fact will, then the concept lives within you, and since it lives it is not possible that it also not live. This {being able not to will} first enters the picture in order to differentiate the image of the merely formal life from its content and thereby to give it form. That which is capable of also not willing is your I. But such an I does not in fact exist, nor does its predicate; instead, it exists in mere reflection. In the second *case*, {you do not will what you ought}, and since you were unable to will, you also did not do so. You are in fact not the image of the dynamic and living concept, | for if you were so, you would have willed without further ado. Instead, you are merely an image *of its image*, {an image} of a concept that is merely formal and ideal. You know what you ought to do and what, God willing, will come to life within you, but at present it has not yet attained actual life. Hence, you do not will and are capable of not willing. Through this "I could," you are merely affecting the postulated life in an image, because at present you are as such still an empty image.

Further, such a theory [of illusion] is immoral and is the true principle of all immorality. This self-sufficient power, what is it really? [It is] the power of resistance, of tearing oneself loose and stubbornly positing oneself as one's own I. Were it not for the sake of this resistance, and for some kind of fame in case you do not resist, why would you reserve for yourself this capacity for resistance? Why would you not let the power of the concept prevail in you in a pure way, so to speak, on your own responsibility?

In order to describe this more precisely, one can understand the basic principle [*Grundsaz*] of the theory of ethics in this way: the I must appear to itself as being merely an appearance, for it ought not to be its own life, but rather the life of something other, something different, i.e., of the concept. [The I is] never its own will or life, but rather [it is] merely the appearance and visibility of the concept, which takes the place [of the I]. The I possesses only the passive observation of [the concept's] arising and of its being. |

Thus the claim that is often asserted elsewhere holds good: through himself a human being is capable of nothing [and] cannot make himself moral but rather must await the breaking forth of the divine image within him.[3] This belief in {one's own ability} and the opinion {that a human being becomes moral on his own} are instead the most certain indications that [the divine image] has not yet emerged and are the greatest obstacles to its doing so, for they

---

3. HALLE: There is nothing good in the I. The I must completely vanish; it must be transformed into a passive appearance that empties itself [*leidend abfließendes Erscheinung*]. There is no hint of morality prior to that (IV/6, 108).

StA 321 [constitute] obstinacy {against the true life}. | All vain pride {must be} cast down. {We must} clearly recognize that there is nothing good within us that is under our own power.

Regardless of whether or not guilt is abolished [as a result], no one should be spared condemnation, nor should any spare themselves from it.

Why not? And, given such a characterization, what is supposed to become of all our teachings, exhortations, and blandishments, as if human beings could [make themselves good] when they [in fact] cannot? Answer. In order to acquire life, the concept must appear first in images, particularly in images of itself, and this is the way [to accomplish this]. Of course, one provides no assistance to one's own power through such representations, but perhaps [one does provide assistance] to the *power of the concept*. Thus, those to whom God has granted it should by all means continue to teach and exhort as strongly as they can, not sparing the most vivid images of contemptibility and nullity or of the magnificence of true being.

Lecture 13

(July 20, 1812)

The exact task {has been} presented, i.e., to describe completely the phenomenon of the true I, the very [I] that here is the life of the concept.

It is not hard in itself to create a determinate image [of the true I] for yourself, though this is a new concept in [this] treatment of the theory of ethics.

The life of the concept = I. Conversely, every I {=} the life of the concept. {This} is the true I. Here {the I} is *immediately* {the life of the concept} in its immediate entry into an image. Elsewhere, {it is only an image}, *its image*.[1] This is the antithesis. Here we want only to become familiar with the concept to the extent that it is *immediately* an image. Thus, in our derivation [*Herabbestimmung*] of its phenomena, we are talking only about how this immediate image shapes itself further in the entire system of its character as an image [*Bildmässigkeit*]. |

(1) {Allow us} to first of all understand this antithesis between indirectness and immediacy in a precise way.

(a) First of all, {that the I is indirectly an image means} that, beyond actual appearance, the concept takes on the form of an image and this mixture appears within actual appearance and in its center, | i.e., in the I. In this case, for those of us who see through it, the concept *is* appearance, and this is its life (just as there is indeed no other objective

---

1. CAUER: The difference is that in the theory of ethics we have the *immediate entry* of the concept into life; in every other place it is only the life of an image, and thus the concept enters life only *indirectly*.

being but the reflection of the life of the concept). But [the concept] does not appear *as such*. The I is not revealed as the life of the concept, and is not moral.² Or, [second:]

(b) The concept, *in just the way it takes on the form of appearance* simultaneously is reflectively aware of itself as taking on [this form]. Therefore, it does not enter this form beyond actual appearance as we said previously but rather within [actual appearance].³ Formerly, its apparent life lacked reflective awareness of itself up to a certain point, instead [having] only its appearance; here, it is reflectively aware of itself immediately. But the center of actual appearance is *always* the I, [which is] the center and synthetic point of unity. In the former case the appearance is not moral, is not the appearance of the life of the concept, but rather is its *dead* corpse, its dying off into a form, regardless of the fact that this death or dying off nevertheless is alive [in appearance].

In the second case, the actual appearance is immediately that of the life of the concept. Still, it is obvious that this actual appearance necessarily enters as such into the whole systematic form of appearance, precisely with this characteristic feature.

Here is the situation. Concept $B \times I\, a + b + c$, etc. as in the form I {in both cases}. The difference is just | *where and at which point* the actual reflection begins. [If it is] genuinely in the I, {then we have} moral appearance. Otherwise, the opposite [is the case], regardless [of the fact] that it is the concept. According to this relation, either $B \times I\, a$, etc. or $B \times a\, I$ or $B \times a + b = I$, etc. The *identity* here is that the concept of b proceeds into actuality.⁴ The *differ-*

---

2. CAUER: The concept that is already enveloped in an image enters actuality in the I. This is an instance of *indirectness*—for us who see this process the appearance of the life of the concept is also [taking place] here, though in a hidden, muddled manner—dressed in a cloak [*gekleidet in die Hülle*].

3. CAUER: Everything that comes to pass does so in the domain of appearance, not in the background.

4. CAUER: The concept enters into a, b, c in the basic form I. It deposits *itself* as life within appearance. The immediate exhibition is in the I—as the life of the I. B is determined through the I but proceeds through $a + b + c$. But the concept appears in a and from that arises once again an I. This is immorality. So too in both remaining forms that distance themselves ever further from morality.

ence lies in whether {it does so} as such, or with formal determinations.[5]

(2) Now it is clear that, if the concept immediately as such enters actual appearance, according to the formula $B \times I$, it will nevertheless take on all the forms of actual appearance (a, etc.) only in this *basic form*. | And so this is the meaning of our task: to accompany this appearance $B \times I$ throughout this series. It is likewise clear that we will see immorality in each form via *antithesis*, in case the form I is not present. This theory of the appearance | of the moral I, through every stage of the world of appearance, becomes at the same time the theory of the appearance of its antithesis, immorality. All that is assumed in order to carry out this task correctly and without error is our familiarity with the forms $a + b$.

(It is clear that we are restricting ourselves purely to the form, in that we are considering the concept purely as such in abstraction from its content.)

To the point.

The life of the I is *freedom*, i.e., indifference with respect to the life of the concept. In the actuality of appearance it is an individual [*eigenthümlich*] life that is able both *to will* and not [to will] vis-à-vis an ought. [This is] a life that stands over against the *life of the concept*, which bears only an ideal form and whose life force reaches only as far as a law or an *ought*.

This is simply how the causality of the concept appears. It takes on this form. The I, as the life of the concept, cannot appear otherwise.

But there are two cases. Either the *indifference* is merely an appearance, or it is a *reality*, though of course within appearance. [Assume that] the I is *in fact indifferent*. In that case it must in fact be so (for appearance). The concept must therefore enter [appearance] in a representational [*bildlich*] form. It {cannot} live immediately but

---

5. [Fichte's marginal note:] *I*, etc. This is the difference. Thus the formula is $B \times I \times a + b + c$ or $B \times a \times I \times b + c$ or $B \times a + b$. Task. The appearance of the concept in the I.

StA 325   rather can only be deposited dead in an | image.⁶ B x a. In this case, the I is *real*; in the other case it is a *mere appearance*, irrespective of the fact that in the former case it is not initially appearance but rather only in fact an appearance of appearance. {(}What, according to this usage, does real or actual mean? This is important for our system, and in general it is good to know in order to put an end to certain confusions concerned with usage. Nothing but God is real. Here, we consider the concept as *real* and hold to this. This {means the same as} *absolute*. This is true also in this case, to the extent that we are assuming that we are occupying an absolute standpoint. Relative reality is discovered everywhere that, from this standpoint of actuality, appearance ceases and, in antithesis to it, its absolute invisibility is discovered.⁷)

In which image {is the I} absolutely {a real principle}? Here we {connect up with} results of other inquiries (a procedure that will be allowed by you, who listen to everything and who are studying from a pure interest in philosophy, and by me, for I admit that I am teaching on the basis of my own insight [*welches Verfahren bei Ihnen, u. bei mir, de rich bekannt bin aus eigener Einsicht zu lehren, u. Sie {, die} aus reinem Interesse für Philosophie studirend, wohl alles hören {, gestattet ist}*]). The I is a principle that creates

II/13, 343   time from itself. |

Therefore, if some time elapses between the appearance of the concept in its clarity to the point of action and the willing [of the concept] in appearance, then the life of the

---

6. CAUER: But this indifference is either a mere appearance or reality. In itself the I has no life. Were it in fact indifferent, it would not be indifferent via its own life but rather through the hidden life of the concept. Thus, the concept would immediately enter into the form *a* and thus first of all into the I. This dying off would be the reason why the I would be indifferent; the I would be the appearance of the image of the concept—of the concept in the image form *a*; and to this extent there would belong to it a true indifference.

7. CAUER: As is well known, only the Absolute is real and exists in fact. We are not occupying this standpoint but rather the standpoint of the image of the absolute; this obtains as absolute for us. Now we are talking about another reality. This is none other than relative [reality]. It exists everywhere that appearance ceases.

concept has not entered [appearance], rather only a mere image of it [has done so]. In the latter sense of reality the I does not merely appear as indifferent with respect to the life of the concept but is so in fact and in truth. The time that intervenes is null [*nichtig*] for the life of the concept; to that extent, it is the appearance of the nullity [*Nichtigkeit*] of the I.

Lecture 14

(July 21, 1812)

StA 326

{A new} criterion of morality {follows} from this point: the *I must appear as immediately willing,* | *as the concept has only been clarified up to the point of willing*; practical clarity and the act of will must occur at a single stroke. If *time* elapses between these, then the I is not moral. Such an {elapsed} time is absolute immorality. The I is null within this *empty time that is unfilled by the life of the concept.*[1]

(The time that follows successively, not the time that is *lost*, which is nothing, is an indication of nullity.)

To me this is the primary intention, the essential characteristic [*Grundzug*] of morality, [namely,] that the attainment of rightness [*Richtigkeit*] and the elevation to clarity are formally the same. Kant did not bring this about, though he without doubt [provides] the most excellent [account] of this material and therefore [spared] no effort.[2]

(1) If no time intervenes between the appearance of the concept in its practical clarity and the act of will, and both exist at a single stroke, then time is entirely filled by the concept alone and by nothing else. We could also therefore

---

1. HALLE: If no time at all occurs between the appearance of the concept in its complete practical clarity and the willing of it, then time is completely filled by the concept. Then the concept is itself a creator of time. That the concept is clear means that it has reached the point of realizability [*Ausführbarkeit*] (IV/6, 111).

2. [Original:] Das ist mir die HauptAbsicht, den Grundzug der Sittlichkeit, das formale derselben, in Richtigkeit zu bringen, u. zur Klarheit zu erheben; wie es selbst durch Kant, ohne Zweifel den treflichsten in dieser Materie, nicht geschehen ist, u. drum keine Mühe {sparen}.

present this as a criterion of the true, moral I, [namely,] that all of its time is completely constituted by the concept alone [*ganz allein durch den Begriff gemacht werde*]. [Put differently,] there is no [time] for such an I but that in which the concept is posited in ever higher degrees of clarity throughout its progressive development. I said [that] all of [the I's] time [is filled]. In doing so I assumed something, namely, that willing does not immediately follow clarity just once in the case of a particular expression of the concept, but rather [it does so] *always* according to a factual law. The I ought to be able to be certain, on account of its appearance to itself, that it could never be otherwise in all eternity.

The regular determination according to which time is filled at any given point is the personality and actuality of the I that we are talking about.[3] That is, what we are discussing here is | the appearance of the I, of the true I, regardless of the fact that we grant and assume that no I exists, but rather only the appearance | of a life that transcends it. To what do we want to link the actuality and reality of such an I? Previously, we have seen that the I, as the apparent life of the concept, is a principle of time. The concept itself is outside of all time, though when it assumes a life, it assumes the form of time and in this way the individuated life that it self-sufficiently deposits appears as a principle of time. This would be the first point. This time can be filled *in a different way* according to the manner of the inner life of the concept depending on whether it lives in a pure way or has died off into an image. Up till now, we have seen that it can either be filled by doing *nothing*, despite the fact that the task [*Aufgabe*] is present, or [it can be filled] by the willing of the concept. This produces two different appearances of the I. The I is always identical to itself *as an I* (this is part of the fundamental concept [of an

---

3. HALLE: The regular determination according to which time is filled up to a presumed point is the personality and actuality of this very I about which we are speaking. They are all I's, distinguished only according to the law on account of which time is filled by them. Here we are only talking about the true I, which is merely the life of a higher concept—this [higher concept] first enters the form of the I insofar as it appears as constituting a time (IV/6, 111).

I]), and so too in its filling of time. The one, moral I alone is actually posited as an I, and remains identical to itself for all eternity, in that its time elapses only in the appearing of the living concept, and nothing else intrudes. The other, [immoral] I [is posited] such that its time [is filled with an] empty consciousness of the concept, without acting in accord with it at all.[4] This would be the second point.[5]

To conclude, the I ought to appear as the life of the concept. In other words, as we now see, it ought to appear as the absolute principle of all of its time, not [just] in *particular*, *individual* times. Whether or not [the I] *wills* in a given case is a matter of its factual self-consciousness. This is a consciousness of an accident, not of its substance or of its stable character. [The I] ought to know that it is going to will for all *time*, that all of its time will not *belong to it* but rather to the life that is unfolding itself within it, and that an actual indifference toward the concept will never intrude.

There are two questions. (a) Is there such a consciousness? And (b) what is it for | an individual?[6] *Ad* (a): of course, {there must be such a consciousness}; this is a consequence of the analysis of the basic principle that has

---

4. CAUER: If it is an I, then the I must remain identical to itself for all eternity, each one in its manner.

5. HALLE: (2) This time can always be filled out in different ways depending on the concept that lies in the background and according to the distinction of whether or not it is living. [It can be filled out] either through inert and indifferent persistence [*Verharren*], or through willing the concept. In this way two different appearances of this form, which is nevertheless always the form of the I, would arise. A genuinely individual I is always supposed to be identical to itself and thus identical in its filling of time. We are positing the I as a universal form. Yet, there is a particular, personal [I]. This distinctness of the actual, personal I is based on the *manner of the filling of time*. This principle is being applied here universally, from the highest standpoint. But it is quite certain that the two I's that are opposed to one another here are distinct according to [the manner] of the filling of time. In the true I, time, which the life of the concept constitutes in an immediate way, drains away. In the second I, time is, on the contrary, constituted by the mere image of the concept. The I, if it is an I, must remain identical to itself for all eternity, each in its own manner (IV/6, 111–112).

6. CAUER: Here there are two questions: (1) Is there such a self-consciousness for all eternity? And (2) How would it look within appearance?

been proposed [at the beginning of the lectures] (and we could not demonstrate it here in any other way—it can only be demonstrated by means of the fact itself and for one who possesses [this consciousness]). The I ought to appear as the life of the concept. But the I is the principle of all time. Thus, the concept ought to appear in the I as the principle of all time, and this should no longer be subject to any fluctuation or change. This alone is the appearance of morality, simply [*schlechthin*] nothing else besides. Ad (b): How {is this consciousness formed}? As a *will* that is seized [*gefaßte*] once and for all, for all eternity. As it is said, I will my duty absolutely; I will it in its pure form. This is how this consciousness is expressed. I do not now know how my duty will be articulated [*aussprechen* wird] in all eternity. But, I have at the present moment anticipated willing it, however it might be articulated, in the single act of willing to constantly do my duty.[7] Particular acts of will must proceed from and develop out of this single [act of will] | for all eternity as accidents of it, just as the particular shape of any duty must be developed out of a concept of duty as such, for all eternity.

All future freedom and every [future] determination of the will are hereby made absolutely impossible.[8] If something is made apparent as a duty, then the I that is being assumed here does it as a consequence of the one eternal self-determination to do just such a thing. All empty time is cancelled [*aufgehoben*]. Clear knowledge and action always exist at a single stroke, with necessity.

This single will, which is substantially and in a purely formal manner directed at duty regardless of its content, is, as we know, not the product of the I but rather the appearance of the concept, [the product] of [the concept's] making itself into such an I. But this guarantees the eternity of the I. Is such an I capable of changing its will during the course of time? Of course [it would be], were it the will of an I!

---

7. CAUER: The particular act of willing *ABCD* is here undertaken for all eternity [*auf all Ewigkeit mit befaßt*] and develops out of the one act of will as its *ACCIDENT*.

8. CAUER: No DELIBERATING or meditating can occur; rather, all of time is filled with the lawful unfolding of duty.

StA 329 But [the moral will] is the appearance of the one absolute concept, which is eternally identical to itself and | exists in no time. Were the will changed at some point, this would only be proof that it was never there, and that one had merely imagined it through some error of judgment.

Lecture 15

(July 22, 1812)

Formula: The true I must appear to itself with an absolute will [to do its] duty, which absolutely cancels [*aufhebt*] all particular acts of will. (This will has to be its personality or character, from which alone it lives, and all the rest of its life flows forth merely as the appearance of this character.) This will can ever be canceled without the annihilation [of the true I], for it is its true being.

{We will make this clear} by way of the antithesis. It could so happen that the I that has been presented up to this point is of two characters, that it gives form to its empty time by persisting in the bare consciousness of an image even once the concept *has pushed through to life*. The latter is a *single occurrence*. Should it be attributed to the I? Is it in accord with its character? No, since it is something new that does not occur in accord with its regular determination. Here again [in this case] there are two [further] cases [that are possible]: either the concept breaks through with its substantial life on this occasion and reveals itself as the eternal, formal will previously described (in which case the I that is presupposed is created anew and becomes something new; the old [I] is annihilated and extinguished, and everything that has been said up to this point holds true for [the I] henceforth); or, after | performing this action [the I] falls back into *indifference*. In this [latter] case (1) the action is like an accident that does not belong to the character [of the I]; it cannot attribute it to *itself*, rather {it must attribute it} to an alien force. (We will make a remarl about this.) | (2) [The action was not performed] for the sake of duty; {thus it was} in no way *morality*. [Morality] is just the one [concept] that assumes its form in life, not an accidental appearance.¹

Morality {must be} an eternal, inextirpable character, otherwise it does *not* exist. {Thus there are} no {individual} moral actions or the like, {rather only *a single*} moral life. Any exception proves that it does not exist.

Consider the matter now from the point of view of the first formula. I say that in this state *a real* and actual I is not present. The appearance that is being investigated can therefore also be articulated in the following way: the I must be completely annihilated. [The I] does not exist, for the concept, as it appears, forms through itself the will and the action. The whole intuition is thus [a matter of] passively watching the life of the concept, without any I that enters into the thread of this sequence and somehow sustains it or carries it forward.²

Since everything comes down to understanding this [point], I want to present it even more clearly to you in a

---

1. CAUER: *Antithesis*. The concept could also push through [just] once to its own life in the second, indifferent I; we must evaluate this as a single occurrence that does not belong to the I, [as] something new—outside the regular determination. But what we have wanted is an I whose character and regular determination is morality; otherwise it is not a moral I. But if the one absolute will actually arises in the second I, then a completely different I steps into its place—the personality of the previous [I] is annihilated. In the other case, where the I falls back into its old indifference after the occurrence of the concept, this must be considered to be something extraordinary, like a sudden intrusion from an alien power; indeed, this is how it appears. Further, morality would not truly be willed—for this must be an eternal, inextirpable character or else there is no morality. Thus there are no individual moral actions. *Being moral* is not the product of an accident—an action—but rather only of a substance, an I. There is no moral action but rather only a *moral life*.

2. CAUER: Let us now consider the matter on the basis of an antithetical formula. The I must be completely annihilated; an I must not exist. The concept must be preeminent as an eternal self-creator—what belongs to the concept occurs immediately as the will of the I and as its effect in the sensible world; an I that carries forward or sustains this series does not occur. An appearance of the I like the one described is absolutely certain of its eternal imperishability—it does not expect it but rather possesses it immediately in each moment. [. . .] Here, there is no distinction between time and eternity such as one commonly makes; rather such an I is itself taken up into the eternal series of time.

remark. An appearance of the I like the one described is immediately certain of its absolute eternity and imperishability. It neither has faith nor hopes, nor does it expect [these], but rather possesses [this certainty] immediately in each present moment. According to its personality, [the I] is itself nothing but the *life* of this absolute concept that develops itself progressively for all eternity; [the I] therefore [develops] with it, since it is indeed nothing else at all besides this life. What [such an I] is in each moment only exists and possesses reality in relation to an infinite progressive development, and without this relation it is unable to exist. Therefore, at each moment it has comprehended the whole infinity and actually possesses the germ of all future time that itself develops, and [the I] develops along with it, since {the concept} only exists temporally within it. I said that the personality [of the I] endures eternally, for [the I] is eternally just the concept | on account of its absolute will. For [the I] {there is} no *other* life; rather, {there is} only the continuation of one and the same [life]. {There is} no distinction between time and eternity. [The I] has already actually entered into absolute eternity, i.e., into the series of time that is absolutely incapable of coming to an end. (Incidentally, this is not a new doctrine: to have the power to have life from oneself; whoever does God's will never dies.)[3] On the other hand, every I that does not appear to itself this way can be certain of the absolute annihilation of his personality | and the best that he can hope for and expect is precisely this annihilation and the emergence of the new, absolutely eternal life of the concept that we are discussing. His life is mortal, plain and simple [*schlechthin sterblich*]; it carries death within itself because it is not a genuine life. We do not know whether this mortality will always transition into a new life or into the absolute vanishing of his appearance from the system of appearance. Still, we have no demonstrative reason against the latter assumption and it can be warranted. We only know that each of us who has the life of appearance must act

StA 331

II/13, 347

---

3. Fichte seems to be paraphrasing several passages from the Johannine corpus in the New Testament, for example, John 10:28 and 11:26.

as if he were destined for true life and therefore consider himself in this manner. Each [person] will discover how it is in his own case at his own time. (The sought for proof of immortality. There is no *universal* [proof]. Each person, however, can know immediately how things stand with him. He looks into his self-consciousness. [Is the] absolute will [present], or not? But for whoever longs for this immortality in the right way, according to {how it is depicted}, this longing is [itself] a pledge [of immortality]. Perhaps one can awaken this longing in human beings through instruction.)[4]

I must make another far-reaching comment here. I hope that it will be intelligible in the brevity with which I am here going to express myself. To contradict the claim asserted [here] under the pretense of religion and morality is a matter of greater irreligiosity and | immorality, and more effectively promotes the latter. (1) {This holds if} one grants (simply because one must) that there is such an absolute sanctification of the will and that it is possible, just not in this life; rather, it is withheld for another [life]. In this life human beings could {attain this sanctification} only as, at best, an *exception*, or else not at all, and can only long for it. [Those who say this] cannot produce an *a priori* proof for this assertion. {Such a proof would} only be possible on the condition of the {presence} of a distinction between how this life appears versus [how] every other life [appears], which they simply do not possess. {They have this insight} only on the basis of experience. Indeed, since they cannot gaze into the hearts of others, external evaluation is guided by their own maxims, on the basis of their own [hearts], which only proclaim that *they* are not [sanctified]! This is how it is. The devotions of this type [of person] always begin with a public confession of their own sinfulness, deep horror, etc. [The way they think of themselves] could be

---

4. HALLE: But everyone that believes himself to be alive must be regarded such that the true life could still break through in him. The immortality of all only exists in morality. There is no universal proof of immortality that is valid for all. Each must gaze within at his absolute self-consciousness. If you do not have the [moral] will, then you have the pledge of death. The drive to immortality is the silent compulsion of the concept, and as far as I can conceive, this longing is a pledge to the one who longs after it that he will obtain it. One should awaken this longing in a human being (IV/6, 114).

true, but it could also not be true, and they could be doing themselves an injustice just for the sake of their maxim that one [only] pleases God if one properly debases oneself before Him. I would then like to know where their famed humility, religiosity, and morality lie when they, without in the meantime reflecting on what they are doing, assert that no human being could be better | than they are, and that their depravity is not somehow an infirmity of their individual nature but rather a universal law. They are not humble at their own expense but rather at that of the human species. Still, granting that they have it right—not regarding an absolute law, which is, as is recalled earlier, inaccessible to them—but rather insofar as up till now no human being that has lived has attained this absolute will—still, what use it is to preach it, inculcate it, or even talk about it? What if what they are doing is merely inculcating as a criterion that no one who is not moral takes himself to be so, while letting the possibility [of sanctification] remain, | just as we too have done (whoever sins once {is still immoral}, etc.; but he does not despair, he gets up and perhaps a new birth takes place)? But they deny [the possibility] so completely in order to block vain striving and to bring human beings to the point that they are satisfied with their wretchedness as the universal destiny, and yet believe that they are thereby offering God the sacrifice of humility. I regard that as pernicious. On the contrary, this is what I think is right: to present the ideal in all its sharpness, clarity, and determinacy, in as lively and animated a way as one can, in order to enflame human beings' striving to equal it (as the situation is different with respect to attaining it). That is the only thing that human beings can do for [other] human beings; indeed, it is the highest.

Lecture 16

(July 23, 1812)

That the human being is nothing, and that, to the extent that he has a reality in appearance, the latter is vanity and pure immortality, sin, and ruin; that no one can give himself new birth into morality, just as little as he could give birth to himself in the sensible world; and that this must occur through the power of the concept or of God—[all] this I understand just as deeply as anyone does, and I have striven to present it to you clearly. There is no dispute about any of this. But God works in accordance with the laws of the appearance of an I, for He steps in [*tritt er ein*] only in concepts and not as an incomprehensible mechanically acting thing; to think otherwise would be idolatry and blasphemy. But the fundamental law of an I is freedom; therefore, what God or the concept effects must immediately appear as effected through one's own freedom (irrespective of the fact that one of course knows that this is only an appearance, not the truth). Furthermore, the determining grounds of freedom are concepts, representations | and instructions that must likewise stand in some comprehensible connection with the determination of freedom. One would have to say this to a human being: you must seem to be at work on yourself (or also: you must be at work on yourself) in an intelligent way; then God is at work on you and carries out his work in you. But [my opponents] abjure this freedom and intelligence and | indicate the use of means that are supposed to produce sanctification in a mysterious and simply incomprehensible manner. This is wrong and confirms a human being in his lethargy, and [it] robs him of the clarity that is the vehicle of all morality, regardless of whatever holy authority or pretext on which this is done. That which is unintelligible and contrary to freedom is sinful and immoral, wherever one believes that it has been discovered.

One can tolerate superstition so long as it remains merely an empty speculation; but if it becomes practical and hinders someone from the use of the correct and true means for the sake of using some magical means, then tolerance would be a betrayal of the cause of humanity.

{The objection is heard that there is a lot that lies} beyond reason that still is not contrary to reason. This meaningless formula is simply repeated to others. First of all {"reason" here would have to mean} *understanding*, laws of thought. In any event, the assertion that a relation or connection is *beyond* understanding is directly *contrary to it*, since the concept, as an image of lawfulness and coherence, should be completely clear, comprehensible, and transparent to itself.[1]

That this nonsense has yet to cease is due to the fact that one does not understand. Hence, I wanted to provide this contribution to the understanding. For me, there are no magical means of formation [*Zauberbildung*].

I want to describe the antithesis more precisely. The *bare*, dead concept emerges as the I; the I is therefore to be understood | as creating its own time. For the present, since we still do not have a particular principle for filling time, we have only an empty time, without life, will, or action. This is the phenomenon of *indifference* [*Gleichgültigkeit*], of having died away to goodness [*Erstorbenheit für das Gute*].

It is clear from the system that the concept can appear in this way, that there is such a stage in its development. One can therefore say that the natural human being, = the I as something real, has become dull and died away to goodness. He understands it well enough, but he is averse to it, closing it off for himself as if it were nothing, and goes

---

1. HALLE: If a sophist uttered something like this a thousand years ago, one simply repeated it. Here the discussion is not about reason but rather about understanding, about the concept of relation (IV/6, 116).

about his way. And yet this is the best that one can say for him. Later on a principle of resistance is joined to this. One can assume that the concept always passes through this stage whenever it develops. Why? {The reason lies in} the form of visibility, such that the concept becomes visible in its particular production of a life and has a *terminus a quo* as well as an antithesis. It is simply incomprehensible why it perseveres for so long at one point in this series, for here we are not discussing a law of the connection between facts | but rather an absolute fact that first provides the understanding with something that needs to be comprehended in the connection.[2]

Occupy the standpoint of a *particular* moral command and relate to it the two appearances of the I that have been described, while assuming that even the latter one wills and carries out what is commanded. It is obvious that, for the first [appearance of the I], which already possesses the absolute will to will its duty as it expresses itself, the particular ought that accompanies this content X is only a | ground for the cognition of what is to be willed but is in no way a motive or an impetus [of the will]. No act of will takes place in time for [a will] that is already directed toward every duty (being thereby directed also at this [particular duty]). On the other hand, with regard to the I that has a different shape, willing does occur [in time] and does so in consequence of the ought that accompanies this content. [This act of will] is something new that runs counter to the regular determination of the I, as has already been shown. This, therefore, is the double meaning of the ought: the ought in its pure universal form is always the object of the moral will, but wherever the ought of a particular content becomes a motive of the will, it is clear that the universal good will does not yet exist. A series of the first type is the uninterrupted effluence [*Abfluß*] of the progressive development of the concept. A series of the second type, in the case that it exists, has discrete moments that are shaped by the indeterminacy and difference [*Differenz*]

---

2. HALLE: The connection must be capable of being understood; not so FACTICITY itself, which is inaccessible to the understanding (IV/6, 116).

of the I and through the causality of the ought that overturns and annihilates these. The will eternally [*in aller Zeit*] *comes to be* in a progressive way, because the indifference of the I endures eternally. But this indifference is something immoral; hence, [in this case] the I is not the pure life of the concept. There is an eternal annihilation of the I, the creation of something new, a continual striving. This is how Kant described morality, and he was incorrect in so doing. For this reason, some other things, such as the doctrine of immortality, had to remain obscure for him, as he may have indicated in his theology, which is the weakest part of his philosophy. In the series that we have presented, the will no longer comes to be, [rather] it *is*, and only alters its accidental features. Thus, the *ought* was only a motive at one time and does not recur for all eternity.[3] |

---

3. CAUER: The concept appears in the form of an *ought*. The absolute will that has been described is immediately directed at the sheer ought [*das blose Soll*], in abstraction from all particular content. Without this formal character of the ought, the absolute will would have no object and would not be a determinate willing. But later on we said that there is no *ought* for the properly moral will, [and that] it would be a sign of immorality if the will still had to be impelled by an *ought*. This is the place to show the different meanings of an *ought*. Let as assume a particular command of duty = X. Both forms of the I comply. For the genuinely moral I this particular *ought* is not a motive, for its will is already [determined] for all eternity and X has already been co-willed in the absolute willing. The particular ought is here only a ground for cognition. The will is no longer in time, and the absolute willing has cancelled all future willing. The situation is completely different with respect to the I of the second shape. Here the absolute will does not yet exist. An act of will comes to be only as a result of the ought that accompanies the content X. Willing here *comes to be* as something new and contrary to the regular determination of the I. This, therefore, is the double meaning of the ought: the ought in its *universal form* must be distinguished from the ought of a *particular content*; if the latter becomes a motive, then the universal good will does not yet exist. In the first series there is a flow, without any moments—the second, were it to exist, would be an eternal annihilation of the I and a creation of something new. This is how Kant presented morality, and in that respect at least he was incorrect. In the first series only the accidents are altered—but in the latter there is an eternal *becoming* of the will.

Lecture 17

(July 24, 1812)

StA 337
II/13, 351

Let us proceed further in our accompanying of the moral will on down through the system of representationality [*Bildlichkeit*].

As the life of the concept, the I is not only the ground of a formal time, of the starting point of a succession, but rather it fills out time with a product [that is produced] from itself, that is, with the likeness of the concept in the objective world. I now want to grasp this distinction precisely. The concept is in itself a pure image, closed and complete in itself. Only by taking on a life in consciousness, by becoming an I, does it acquire a likeness. Its I-form [*IchForm*] is therefore the reason why it must obtain an objectivity, a likeness. Therefore, one can say in general that the I is the ground of an objective world and thus of the filling of time [*Zeiterfüllung*].

(I said earlier that the concept is complete in itself, something that is clearly and definitely articulated [*ausgesprochnes*], closed, to which nothing is to be added and that needs nothing else outside of itself. Whence and for what purpose is this need for an object that corresponds to it? Why is it not sufficient to comprehend the supersensible cognitively and to have, by so doing, at least produced its image? Why also do something? [The answer is the] *life* of the concept, which brings along with itself the fact that it is an absolute life. But [the concept] is life only in the form of the I, of self-consciousness (or reflective awareness, as

I presented it yesterday in the *Logic*).[1] It is *life*, in no way *death*; it must never be deposited in a closed form—hence [it is] something *infinite* that *progressively cognizes* itself. Hence its object must be given to it, because it is only in that way that life is brought to a standstill in order to recur once again in a new form, as life. The new [form] only occurs after the completion of the next task.) |

This is the I as the actual life of the concept, the moral [I]. But the life of the concept has to occur at some time in consciousness as something that emerges [*entstehend*], i.e., as the I that is already *active efficaciously in an objective way*, transforming its objective creations into the instrument of the concept. The I (not yet as the life of the concept but rather as its mere image) must not appear to be merely dead, inert, and indifferent, as in the preceding considerations, but rather as in fact acting efficaciously and as being a cause independently of the concept—[being a cause] freely in a genuine sense, out of itself, from itself, through itself. [The I must appear as a] *free, absolute principle through itself.* |

Of course, as is self-evident, such an I is also an image of the concept, [though] not yet of its life. Instead, it is an image of the form of its distinctive life as such.

This much [is said] in order to direct you toward the new sphere of investigation. Now [we will go] deeper into the derivation of the important point. The investigation requires precision [*Schärfe*] and is entirely new; yet, precisely because it is new, it promises a new clarity regarding the entire subject matter.

Beyond *moral consciousness* [we are] familiar with the empirical domain [*die Empirie*]. Now suppose that the whole faculty of sight is *restricted* to the latter. In that case, whatever might be assumed to exist *in itself* beyond the empirical domain would never be capable of coming into view, because there would [in that case] be no faculty for it. Thus, whoever asserts something moral within consciousness [also

---

1. The reference here is to the concurrent lectures on transcendental logic. See GA II/14, 119–121.

thereby] asserts something in particular that lies beyond the ken of the empirical faculty of sight.[2, 3] This faculty of sight is supposed to distinguish the empirical from the nonempirical and characterize both in their opposition. This faculty of sight is a faculty *of the concept*. All of this means (carry out the examination with me) that the absolutely and unconditionally [*schlechthin*] posited faculty of sight carries with itself the concept | of the basic character of the empirical domain, under which it subsumes everything empirical, though this latter is not [conceived of] as the only thing that is visible. Instead, [the faculty of sight] carries with itself the opposing concept of something else that is equally [*gleichfal{l}s*] visible, which would be the nonempirical domain [*das nicht-Empirie*]. The *non*empirical lies beyond this domain [*Gebiete*]. This is sufficient for now [*vor*

---

2. HALLE: Therefore, anyone who asserts something moral within consciousness necessarily also asserts a determinate faculty of sight for morality. The faculty of sight as a whole is thus not restricted to the merely empirical domain. Indeed, the faculty of sight that, in its unity, is supposed to see both the empirical and the nonempirical, would have to be capable of distinguishing both and grasping them in their opposition. This faculty of sight would accordingly be a faculty of the concept of the empirical and of the nonempirical. The faculty of sight, which is simply presupposed, would have to carry with itself the concept or the basic character of the empirical domain, and along with it also the opposed concept of something else that is not the empirical domain (IV/6, 118).

3. CAUER: This side of [*diesseits*] moral consciousness the empirical domain is also well known. Now assume that the faculty of sight as a whole is restricted merely to the empirical domain and, as it were, reckons only on it; yet, much might still exist beyond the empirical domain, e.g., a moral world. Now [the moral world] would never occur [in consciousness], because there would be no faculty of sight for it. If something moral is asserted in consciousness, one necessarily also asserts a faculty of sight for it. This faculty of sight, which is supposed to see the empirical and the nonempirical in their unity, would have to be capable of distinguishing and characterizing both. This faculty of sight would accordingly be a faculty of the concept of [both] the empirical and the nonempirical. This assumed faculty would have to carry with itself the basic characteristic of the empirical domain and of something absolutely opposed [to it] that would also be visible. The result of this would be that the conceivability [of the nonempirical] would be posited independently of all actual appearance—be it only in comparison to the empirical domain. This is presupposed prior to every actual appearance of the concept—the eye—the understanding.

der Hand genug]. The *visibility* and *conceivability* of [the nonempirical] is posited independently of every appearance of the concept, albeit only through the antithesis with the empirical domain. The absolute eye, faculty of sight, or understanding is likewise thus posited as being able to see and cognize [the nonempirical].[4]

All seeing {is} a seeing of sight, a self-seeing [*Alles sehen, {ist} sehen des Sehens, sich sehen*]. All sight is embedded [*niedergelegt*] in reflexivity. The I must be able to see itself as seeing something nonempirical, and since everywhere it only sees itself immediately, {it must} be able to *see itself* as something *nonempirical*. This ability must be absolute, given immediately with factual knowing, and so belongs to universal reflexivity. Of course it becomes further determined within sight but not created.

Now how does this sheer *visibility* of the nonempirical enter into an actual empirical and factual knowing? (Our view is {that it does so}.) What is the principle within the empirical domain through which its insufficiency as the whole of knowing and its connection with something higher is revealed? Historically [*Historisch*]. The empirical domain is the exhibition of representationality [*Bildlichkeit*], simply the visible form of an object | on the basis of a subject as such [*aus einem Subjekte überhaupt*]. This decides the issue. Only one subject is required for [the empirical domain]. How, then, is [the nonempirical] discovered within the empirical domain? A sum of subjects, of I's, a community [*Gemeinde*] of I's is discovered empirically, in a factual way within factual vision, without any contribution from freedom, | and no one can alter it! In this much the fact of the empirical domain exceeds its concept, and it is evident that not only does it make *sight* visible, which it is supposed to do according to its concept, but rather [it makes visible] *something absolutely* [*schlechthin*] *visible* that simply

---

4. HALLE: The pure concept enters into consciousness. We have assumed as much. We knew of no other consciousness. But there is also still an empirical consciousness, and consciousness as a whole must be a faculty for distinguishing the two. This is assumed prior to every actual appearance of the concept. The absolute eye that can see and cognize this determinate [concept] as such—understanding (IV/6, 119).

exists in the form of sight, i.e., a *community of I's*. With this the superempirical [*überempirische*], which is a seeing that is not empty but which actually and in fact has content, is exhibited plainly to all eyes. Each one has to see it; whether everyone understands it as we have described the understanding and concept of it is another matter. Each individual now acquires a *double meaning*. In part, [each] is purely empirical, the exhibition of the empty form of a sight. To that extent [each] is absolutely identical to all the rest, in that the mere form of sight is everywhere identical to itself; one [individual] would suffice. In part, [each] is something in himself, a member of a community. Up to this point only the empty formal being of this [individual] is familiar, not yet its inner and qualitative [being] that can only be made visible in a life, since this alone is the basic form of all visibility. This much, however, is clear, namely, that this community is an organic whole assembled out of such individuals; each individual has his part in the being and life of the community in which no other is absolutely identical to him. [Each individual has] his *individual character*. Thus, like the whole, each individual is something truly real (at least when compared to the empty empirical domain): a real life based on itself [*aus sich selbst heraus*]. We will further investigate how it is that this might be able to appear.

Lecture 18

(July 27, 1812)

(1) The I must be capable of appearing as self-sufficient and as filling out time through itself, {as} a self-sufficient principle of objective representations. [The I must be capable of] this prior to the beginning of the life of the concept within it, because the latter must appear as starting at some point in time. |

Thus, [the I] must appear as a self-sufficient principle of objective appearance from itself, through itself, of itself. The human being must possess a causality, must be capable of living and acting efficaciously in an immoral way, independently of *morality*, otherwise he would not be capable of doing so morally.

(2) Whence is such [a causality] {derived} in the system of appearance known to us? Within the knowing that simply [*schlechthin*] exists, i.e., [empirical] knowing, something must appear that is not capable of being comprehended | on the basis of the concept of the empirical, i.e., that it is the form of pure, empty representationality [*Bildlichkeit*].[1] [What is supposed to appear in this way] must therefore be thought of as something superempirical, as something *visible* in itself, not as mere *visibility*. The community of individuals, and each member of it, is such a thing, for one subject would suffice for the exhibition of merely formal sight.[2]

---

1. HALLE: The concept of the empirical is that the form of sight appears in it, the sight of nothing (IV/6, 120).

2. CAUER: This must appear within empirical knowing. Something would have to appear within it that could not be explained on the basis of the empirical and that therefore would have to be thought of as something superempirical—as something

Every individual is, therefore, something twofold. In part, [each one] is the merely empirical image of a sight, and to that extent all are absolutely identical; the same thing is merely repeated and posited in multiple ways within all. In part, [each one] is a part of what exists actually and *realiter* in the sight, and to that extent is himself something real, namely, a part of *real appearance*.

(3) {The following point should} not be misunderstood: *how* appearance exists is not something that appears in the individual world but rather for the first time in the moral world. Instead, [what appears in the individual world] is [just] *that* it exists, and that something that is not merely sight, but which in itself is invisible, is visible in the sight. It becomes visible precisely in each individual world.[3]

Appearance {is given} in the form of representationality. *Representationality* {means} that something exists in the form of *representationality*.

(4) How, then, does this appear? The I is a principle; therefore, the community of individuals as such, and each individual member of it, must appear within actual appearance as a principle, [as] acting efficaciously in an objective manner.[4] How? Can the I (as I will designate it in general

---

visible in itself. Here "in itself" means not mere sight but rather what is seen. As we have seen, the community of individuals and each member of the same is such a thing.

3. CAUER: (3) Real appearance, at any rate, appears in this individual world, though not *how* it is (as in morality) but rather only *that* it is. The purely empirical domain is an appearance of REPRESENTATIONALITY [*BILDLICHKEIT*] and nothing more. However, in this appearance of ours it is asserted that something is there that lies at the basis of this REPRESENTATIONALITY. The *quality* of appearance of course falls out from REPRESENTATIONALITY, but the *form* of appearance must lie within it.

4. [Fichte's marginal note]: *Important claim*: the real (as opposed to mere *sight*—the relatively real—we know [it is merely] appearance and that in the true sense nothing is absolutely real but God) can only appear within this reality as *being a principle*. Thus, because reality only appears to itself in the form of the I [*IchForm*], as appearing to itself [*als sich erscheinend, sich erscheint*], this I, as the expression of mere sight, appears as *existing* and thus must appear in the opposite, in *reality*, as a principle. [Paragraph break in original] Being a principle in an objective way is therefore just a *form of appearance*, the form of the visibility of appearance as something real. [Paragraph break in original] Its essence in itself can, at any rate, become visible and alive within the I, beyond appearance. The supersensible is actually the *one*, not the *individual*, [it is] the appearance of God. Just as certainly as this appears is it something that holds universally [*gemeingültiges*], that pertains to all, and that is directed toward all.

terms here) appear as *principium essendi* [principle of being] of the objective world? No, for the real does not determine appearance, does not posit it through its determining, but rather is determined by it. Thus, since it is still supposed to appear as a principle, it can only appear as determining it in a further way!

In what manner? (Here we are only recapitulating familiar claims in a different way.) The I, as such and in each of its forms, dissolves analytically [*auflösend, analytisch*] in relation to the manifold of being. | It would therefore have to be a principle in this manifold. But its actually and *realiter* being a principle in [the manifold] | and in relation to it means that it is the author [*Urheber*] of a *new order of the manifold*.[5]

(5) That which is real and what is merely empirical appear within the same factual view and are unified at a single stroke in the very same I. The empirical being and the *real principle* are complete [*fertig*] {at once}. The derivative order of the manifold is therefore one that does not follow from the mere laws of being and cannot be ascribed to [being] but rather only to the I. (Thus, the character of

---

5. HALLE: How then does this real = relatively real appear within appearance? The I would have to appear as real; but the I is a principle. Therefore, the community of individuals as such, and each individual [within it], would have to appear as a principle in actual appearance, as acting efficaciously in an objective way. The real or appearance, as opposed to REPRESENTATIONALITY [*BILDLICHKEIT*], according to our assertion, can only appear in the form of being a principle, because reality only appears as existing in the form of the I. REPRESENTATIONALITY appears as an I. REPRESENTATIONALITY is the way that it exists. The whole I must appear as something limited, simply in itself. A being within a determinate system. It must also appear as something real that exists within REPRESENTATIONALITY. This is the antithesis, and thus [it appears] as being a principle. If this [is the case], then the entire form of being a principle of reality can be nothing but visibility. But can the I somehow appear as *PRINCIPIUM ESSENDI* of the objective world as such? No! The real does not determine appearance, but rather, on the contrary, REPRESENTATIONALITY is what determines the real. Thus, the I as a principle can only appear as further determining the world = as setting itself in motion [*sich regend*] within the existing REPRESENTATIONALITY, for REPRESENTATIONALITY is the basic defining form of appearance. In what manner does this occur? The I as such dissolves analytically in relation to the manifold of being. The I could therefore only be a principle in this manifold. But its being *realiter* a principle in this manifold means: it is the author of a new order of the manifold (IV/6, 121).

a product of nature and that of a product of freedom are distinguished, and each bears its own character that cannot be transferred, confused, or mistaken. Both belong within merely factual knowing; these, therefore, are concepts that are neither acquired nor produced but are rather absolutely original.) {This is an} order that *can* only be attributed to the I.[6, 7]

---

6. CAUER: Accordingly, each member of the community must be exhibited as producing order [*ordnend*] with freedom before it can appear as an organ of morality. In the empirical domain itself the I is given this way. This shows also whence the material of the moral law derives.

7. HALLE: The empirical is a completely bounded whole, and here all are slaves of the law of nature. On the other hand, the I is supposed to be seized by a higher law. Which I? The natural I? The possibility of being seized by a higher law does not belong within the I. Rather, there must be something supernatural within the I as it is given. It is an order beyond nature. Should the moral law occur, a material must already exist. This is the supernatural order as which the I must appear (IV/6, 122).

Lecture 19

(July 28, 1812)

Before the appearance of the moral life can emerge within some individual, the latter is exhibited within actual appearance as a principle of some order, i.e., as a free cause that acts efficaciously.[1, 2]

---

1. CAUER [Note: The transcripts diverge from Fichte's manuscript of Lecture 19 and largely agree with one another. It would appear that Fichte condensed his originally planned remarks somewhat.]: The I that is supposed to be seized by the moral law must appear to itself as effectuating a new order that lies beyond nature. The individual world as a whole, with its effects, is the appearance of appearance itself. The solitary individual [*Einzelne*] does not act efficaciously, but rather it is the appearance that resides in all [that does so]—thus, too, the effect of a solitary individual is cognized by all. All efficacious action is grounded in a concept of an end—in this case it is supposed to be based on a concept of an end of a higher order. Accordingly, the eye for the higher order would have to have already arisen in the individual. The I ought to appear as acting efficaciously—or, more briefly put, the *I ought to act efficaciously* within a completely higher order; a higher order ought to be produced that does not belong within nature. Hence, the I must have a concept of a higher order, which it can only acquire to the extent that it has a concept *of itself*, for the concept of the new order = α belongs within it. Such a concept, however, is itself not possible without the concept of nature = β, which is supposed to be arranged differently [than it is]. The character of the new order is indicated here merely *negatively*. It is an order that is necessitated by the self-sufficiency of the I. To give a provisional example, this is the basis of all aesthetic judgments (see Kant's [*Critique of*] *the Power of Judgment*). This requirement first obtains when the I has flourished up to a certain point [*wo das Ich so weit gediehen ist*].

2. HALLE: This I is not yet moral. We consider the I as it ought to become the instrument of the concept (IV/6, 122).

For this individual and for every other individual, what [he] produces as a principle is a universally valid, objective intuition, since it is the appearance of that which is real in the empirical domain. Bringing about a certain *ordering* is conditioned by the concept of an order of this sort, i.e., the concept of an end [*Zwekbegriff*]. This latter, in turn, is conditioned by the concept of an order that is given within the factual being of the world. Thus, a certain development of the concept necessarily precedes efficacious action.

I have already asserted that [what is produced by an individual] is an *order* that bears the characteristic of the I, of intelligence [*Geistigkeit*], through which the I is manifested in actuality as something self-sufficient and existing in itself, not as | a mere product of the sensible world. Were this not made clear, the whole point of this instruction [*Unterrichts*] would be lost.

The I is, in part, an exhibition of empirical sight, and to that extent [it is] a product of nature [*NaturProdukt*] and a natural thing [*NaturDing*]. Here it is governed by a drive for self-preservation, and it also appears to act as a result of this [drive]. It is in no way free and self-sufficient, nor something in itself, but rather is a natural being. At present we are not going to discuss this efficacious action under the dominance of the natural drive.

[But,] on the other hand, [the I] is in part an exhibition of *that which is real* within appearance. To that extent there is a drive, and so a possible manner of acting, toward an order that does not fall under the law of nature | and is not necessitated [*gefodert*] by it. [This order] simply corresponds [to the I], it belongs within its self-sufficient being and is necessitated by it. (If you desire examples, then peruse Kant's theory of aesthetics in the *Critique of the Power of Judgment*. He makes some very keen observations there and combines them in a clever way, irrespective of the fact that he did not survey the subject [from the perspective of] his whole system.) For the educated, it is better to say, if you please, that the order we are talking about *ought* to exist; and it is presently the educated whom {are being addressed} [*dem gebildeten nemlich: wovon sogleich {die Rede sein soll*}].³

(6) That which is real within appearance is made visible in the appearance of a supernatural order, [one] that is being described here simply in accordance with the law of the nature of a factual knowing as such, which we are familiar with as a law of lawlessness or of fate [*Ungefährs*]. Hence, it would not immediately occur to someone that the I is actually and in fact the principle of this development, but instead that it is only the reflection of the | development of what is invisibly real to the point of visibility, and that this proceeds according to no law. The individual develops first as a merely natural creature [*Naturwesen*] up to the point of [acquiring some] skill in self-preservation. It next [develops] as an I in itself, in accordance with its spiritual nature [*geistigen Wesen*], first of all to a level of cognition of these intellectual concepts and of the purposiveness of nature for them. [The individual] next [develops] to a level of skill in implementing [these concepts]. In this manner, the individual first acquires his individual character, which is something necessarily *spiritual*, on the basis of the sphere of concepts so described. (a) The merely empirical I has no character; [every empirical I] is identical, striving for self-preservation, fleeing from pain, desiring [*wollend*] sensual well-being, at most occupying a standpoint in space and time. (b) Character is not innate to a human being but is developed in time according to incomprehensible causes

---

3. HALLE: Accordingly, the eye for a higher order would have already had to come into being in the individual. [. . .] An order ought to occur in nature that is not possible through the mere law[s] of nature. The task is [laid] upon the I. This would require not only an eye for the world but rather [also] an eye for itself whereby that which is higher in it would arise for it. [. . .] If the I is absorbed in nature [. . .], the I is an animal and a tool. If it elevates itself beyond nature, then goals [*Zwecke*] belong to it that further determine nature. Here, too, the I is not free. It is only the appearance of the higher, intellectual nature; or, the I is the exhibition of that which is real in appearance and thus is a drive for an order that does not correspond to nature but to the essence [*Wesen*] of nature (IV/6, 123).

and laws. The human society that educates itself for concepts does best. It is incomprehensible why this education does not take hold in one case but does in another, or why a different [education] produces different results.

Lecture 20

(July 29, 1812)

(7) As a result of this character, the I is a self-sufficient principle in the objective world for something that expresses its character, independently of the moral law and prior to its awakening. This is because the community of individuals, to the extent that it has developed to this higher spiritual existence, is a self-sufficient principle of such a product, which otherwise would not exist without it, through mere nature. Hence [the community] shows itself to be something other than nature, something that exists in itself, since [nature] is nothing. |

The concept of duty, just in case it appears, has [its] material [*einen Stoff*] in this character and in its material content, | [a material] to which it attaches itself, from which it borrows its own content, and which it further determines.

(7) [*sic*] So much in general and as an overview of the context. Before proceeding further, however, it is necessary to state more definitely the concept of this spiritual order and spiritual end that we have only indicated and of which we have only given a negative description (i.e., as not being an end of nature [*Naturzwek*]).

Let us straightaway take up the matter at its highest point.

In truth, it is the community of I's, of minds [*Geister*], [i.e.,] their unity, that is manifested in the aforementioned supernatural element of factual knowing as a being in itself. In individuals, this [community] is only split apart through the form of consciousness, since, for reasons that will not be discussed here, this community only possesses consciousness indirectly [*mittelbar*] in the form of individual consciousness, never immediately. Therefore it must be manifested as a community. Thus, the only criterion for when the elevation of an individual to *real consciousness* has attained clarity is when it appears to itself as a member of the community, of a totality [*eines Ganzen*] of which it is an integral part. The natural I, on the other hand, regards itself as being alone; the only soul in its universe [*Weltsystems*] (according to the remark made previously, it is entirely correct about this).[1, 2] {The individual as a real consciousness thus appears to itself as} something in itself, yet as a part of the whole and within the order of the whole, for only the whole exists in itself. Hence, when it comes to *concepts*, [the individual] exhibits itself as real only in those that are purely and simply [*schlechthin*] directed toward the community as a whole and that it can only think to the extent that it grasps itself as an image of the whole. Are there such {concepts}? Every scientific insight, to the extent that it is articulated *in a way that obtains universally*, | posits reason as something universal that is identical to itself; and no one understands such a proposition who has not established this identity of reason in itself and cast off all individuality. {Such an insight} is acquired through elevation to laws beyond the fact of appearance, to secure [*sichern*] indicators of their superempirical character. [Mere] appearance, on the other hand, isolates and divides; a determinate object can only be enjoyed and possessed by one [person]; its use is regarded as a common possession. Further, when it comes to *acting* and *having an effect* [*Handeln u. Wirken*], all must have the goal [*Zwek*] of exhibiting the unity of the

---

1. CAUER: The natural I is egoistic—it is alone; this happens because it is merely the exhibition of sight, for which only one I is required. Where EGOISM is broken, the appearance of the real commences.

2. HALLE: Thus, where this intelligence is manifest, the community, the whole, is [also] manifest. If the individual appears to himself as a member of the whole, he is spiritual; that is the only CRITERION for the reality of the I, [namely,] that it knows itself as part of a whole. The natural I considers itself to be alone. The natural I is absolutely egoistic, and rightly so, since it is nothing but the exhibition of the mere form of sight, for which only one I is required. Where EGOISM is broken, the appearance of the real commences (IV/6, 124–125).

II/13, 358

community in appearance, of overcoming [*aufzuheben*] every individual characteristic, i.e., limited measure of insight and skill [*Kunstfertigkeit*], and communicating to all the same insight and skill. Thus, since there is really in all only one character, [the aim should be] the highest intellectual development [*Geistesentwiklung*] in time, which is merely repeated in the distinct | material forces, so that all ever progress [*forthandeln*] toward one single mind [*in Einem Geist, u. Sinne*]. No one must therefore want to keep the knowledge he has obtained to himself, nor to esteem it as *his own private* possession, nor recognize it as something that exists [*u nicht für existent anerkennen*], but should only want it to the extent that all have a share of it. No one should desire that his [knowledge] be his property but rather should strive equally to obtain it and to communicate what he has obtained. This holds likewise for those practical skills [*Fertigkeiten*] that are here concerned with nothing other than this working upon the entire community from each individual point within it.[3] It is obvious that everything destined for this universal communication must be actually intelligible and obtain universally; each retains what is actually individual and sensuous. Community is comprised of a, b, c, d. The sensible existence that is common to all is thereby subtracted. That which is *spiritual* (here think of scientific, lawful thought) breaks through in one of its individual *shapes*, at some moment in time, at least in the one that we are supposed to be | taking into account here.[4]

StA 348

---

3. HALLE: That which truly exists [*Existente*] is appearance (IV/6, 125).

4. HALLE: [The following schema is presented:]

$$\begin{array}{c} G \\ \underline{A\ B\ C\ D} \\ A\ B\ C\ D \end{array}$$

[The text resumes:] In A in a different way than in B or in C. The task is laid upon each that he communicate his intellectual being to all. Therefore, what has broken through in A should not remain there, etc. A would stand separately from B, through acting efficaciously in an invisible way, in the background, etc., and they would not be one. They act in this mind and what belongs within each flows out from each into all. This is simply through efficacious action. In acting efficaciously in an invisible way, the intellectual precipitates something [*setzt sich . . . ab*] in an individual way; in doing so visibly, it precipitates in a unity. This distinction is important (IV/6, 125–126).

The task is laid upon each [individual] to make all others equal to himself and to become equal to them. At some point they cross the threshold [*In einiger Zeit sind sie es darüber*]. This equality [*Gleichheit*] is a matter of their *freedom*, though only of *apparent* [*scheinbaren*] freedom, since what is really at work here is appearance itself.[5]

This gives us some insight into the hitherto unknown content of the concept; it is obvious as to its mere form. Each [individual] can *discover* the qualitative content, as has been properly shown here in a clear way for the first time, within immediate *consciousness*.[6]

(1) The only truly self-sufficient thing within appearance is *appearance itself*, as it is in itself, as the image of God. This exists in its unity as the community of individuals.

(2) This, its being, is exhibited as a *task*, for it appears in the form of an absolute principle. Thus, the concept is necessarily directed toward the whole and speaks of the whole. In a real sense there is no individual duty but rather only one of the *whole* community. This, however, is the bringing forth of a certain world order, which is absolutely incomprehensible, since it must be manifested immediately. Moreover, in this world it does not emerge in some particular consciousness [*irgend einem Bewußtseyn*], partly because the community is not yet complete [*vollendet*], and partly, among other reasons, because it is imperfect and must be continually formed [*gebildet*]. ({I will} then {add} a remark about this.)[7]

(3) This task is not expressed in a collective consciousness, since there is none, but rather in {an} individual [consciousness], in one way in one place and in a different way elsewhere, in accord with an incomprehensible law. It is, however, expressed as a task for the whole. In the first instance, the task is laid upon each individual to commu-

---

5. Fichte's manuscript has a break after this paragraph.

6. HALLE: There is no theory of duty [*Pflichtenlehre*]; rather, each must look within his own breast regarding what he ought to do. There can, however, be a formal description of the concept of duty (IV/6, 126).

7. CAUER: Aside from the *sensuous* drive, an *intellectual* drive also belongs in the I, which contains the entire world that is here described; no morality is as yet visible here.

nicate his perspective [*Ansicht*] to all and to make those of others his own [*sich anzueignen*], to form [*bilden*] himself to the point of harmony with what obtains universally [*gemeingültigen*] within others' [perspectives], while these should do likewise regarding what obtains universally in his. Each [individual] has his own spiritual character in this scenario, but the task is for all to mingle these characters into one, {so that} the whole community is of a single mind [*Sinne*]. Should this goal be obtained at some time [*einmal*], it is but an intermediary [stage] on the way toward the self-exhibition of appearance. Until this is attained, the world order being referred to has not yet been exhibited through appearance; instead [what has happened] is that the bringing forth *of its image* has been worked toward, [something] that itself cannot be complete until the entire community is complete.[8] This is the condition of the human species in this life, and this is what distinguishes it in every case from a future state, i.e., not the fact that [the human species] cannot attain a moral disposition [*Gesinnung*], but rather the fact that it cannot achieve the genuine task of morality. The present life is a preparation; the true, world-creating concept is not given within it, rather what is given is only its image. The object is not given up rather just the formation [*Bildung*] of the individual into an instrument [of the concept]. Each [individual] ought to work upon himself and upon others; he only works upon himself to the extent that he works upon others, and vice versa. This is a *reciprocal interaction* [*Wechselwirkung*] insofar as only what obtains universally is under discussion. This also demonstrates the necessity of the *immortality* of everyone who merely cultivates himself [*sich bilden*] morally. The future life is only possible through the identity of the individuals who give form [*bilden*] to the present, for it consists merely in the application [*Anwendung*] | of what has been acquired here, i.e., in the realization of the image that they have helped to sketch out

---

8. CAUER: That the determinate world order can be produced requires (1) that the quantity [*Anzahl*] of individuals is actually and in fact finite [*abgeschlossen*]; (2) that [the members of] this finite [quantity] of individuals have, as it were, exchanged parts with one another; (3) that a single, collective consciousness of the species has emerged.

here below. No one can err {in the future life}, since each belongs to the whole and to its task as a member. On the other hand, it is evident that those who have learned nothing here below, or who have not developed from themselves anything that obtains universally and eternally, are entirely unsuited for such an order of things. This is the most we can say as a general claim, and it promotes the end of morality to say it. We must, however, restrain ourselves from applying this to any particular individual, leaving it to each one's conscience.

Lecture 21

(July 30, 1812)

II/13, 360 To return again [to the point].[1]

The human being can, in this manner, without any morality, will [something] on the basis of the mere stimulus [*auf bloßen Antrieb*] of the spiritual nature within him. This is the formal criterion for such a will: he wills because he wills, absolutely and unconditionally [*schlechthin*]. He has insight into the truth, and this insight becomes a force for him, a will, something that is carried out [*Ausführung*]. The latter {is} necessary, otherwise he would not even be willing. He *wills*, just because he wills. {This} is the *main point* [to make] for the purposes of the subsequent antithesis. His *willing this* is the boundary of his consciousness, for further than that the concept has not penetrated into consciousness. Perhaps he expresses himself this way: he wills because it is true, right, fitting, or ought to be. But the former [three] are judgments, not motives of the will; with the latter, in case it does not just mean the same as these, he is merely saying that he wills it. It could very well be the case, and indeed we are assuming that it is so, that the true, the right, the proper have become what he wills, have acquired a dynamic, animating [*regen*] life, and that he cannot do
StA 351 otherwise. |

---

1. HALLE: In any event, the essence of this I in itself can become visible within an I. The appearance of the supersensible. This is not the individual [I] but the One, the appearance of God. Just as certainly as it appears is this something that is universally valid. What is rational in itself is the appearance of God (IV/6, 127).

That which he wills is always some condition of the human species, since the concept that has broken through into his consciousness is one that obtains universally and that belongs to the rational community of agents [V{ernun}ftgemeinde handelnder]. Were this not so, then the aim [Zwek] would be sensuous and selfish and would not fall within the scope of our present consideration. [What is willed] could be an order of nature, though [only one that is willed] for the sake of the species, not out of selfishness (e.g., enthusiasm for economy).[2] Or it could be legislation, the state, or art and science, or even religion, [considered] with regard to its theoretical truth and as part of rational knowledge [VftErkenntniß]. Such people possess an inspiring charisma [Begeisterung]; they are heroes, benefactors of the human species, albeit only as blind instruments of some particular concept. This is how I think of many celebrated heroes of history.[3] [For example,] Muhammad, enthusiast for the concept of the oneness [Einheit] of God, full of bitter hatred toward polytheism wherever he believed he had encountered it, who introduced this confession of oneness with fire and sword.[4] Or others, who with fire and sword compelled people to be free or happy in accordance with the way that they had prescribed. They could work wonders and move mountains, but all of that availed them naught, since they did not have love.[5] |

Now, if on the other hand the concept as such breaks through into conscious life, how does appearance turn out? At the stage being described here, life commences with a determinate, qualitative act of willing and is real-

---

2. CAUER: [A] will can indeed be directed at nature, albeit for the sake of the whole human species. For example, a true enthusiasm for agriculture [. . .].

3. It is worthwhile to recall the momentous events of recent months; Napoleon had crossed the Niemen on June 24 and begun the Moscow campaign. It is natural that Fichte's thoughts should turn to the question of how great historical personages stand with respect to morality.

4. HALLE: This is how I think of Muhammad, according to the one-sided presentation of Christians. He categorized Christianity as idolatry and was inspired by the oneness of God (IV/6, 128).

5. Cf. 1 Corinthians 13:2.

ized within it. There is consciousness on this side but not beyond [*Diesseits ist Bewußtseyn, nicht aber jenseits*].[6] The concept (which is all I that we are considering), the act of willing it, and its life coincide internally and are one. {This individual} does not will in accordance with the concept, as a consequence of it, nor does he have it as a motive; instead, he wills unconditionally [*schlechtweg*], as we said earlier, and this act of willing agrees with the concept through an unknown power [*unbekannte Kraft*]. From the standpoint of morality, the concept enters into consciousness, and life is separate and distinct from it. Moreover, life is related to the concept and is considered to be its life, as though nothing else were present aside from its force; between these two elements, which would in that case coalesce into one, a mediating member enters that both divides and unifies, i.e., consciousness, their image of themselves, and their reciprocal relationship. Assuming, then, that this cognition does not remain empty and dead on account of the inner deadness [*Erstorbenheit*] that is posited as being possible according to the earlier point of view, but rather that it becomes vital [*lebendig*] and seizes hold of the will immediately, it would at first seem that life is the same as far as content goes both here and there, [i.e., is] the causality of the concept X, with only the formal difference that the moral [life] is perfectly clear to itself, knows that it does what it does, and why, whereas, on the contrary, the [life] previously described is a blind instrument that is not clear to itself.

I say, however, that the content and goal [*Zweck*] of life as a whole becomes hereby something completely different—this is important to me, and for that reason I have made these precise distinctions and have led up to it so gradually. [The moral individual] conceives clearly that life ought to be the life of the concept as such. He wills (1) as per the previous description, not merely that his life [should] acquire the shape of the concept X that has broken out within him but rather of the concept purely and

---

6. CAUER: There consciousness reaches only the determinate qualitative concept; beyond the concept there is no consciousness.

simply [as such], whose shape he also assumes. The concept as such, determined through its pure form, the ought, is present for him in a representational [*bildlich*] concept. His eyes are therefore opened and ready to cognize [the concept] in whatever shape it appears. {He} does not will X immediately, but rather | indirectly, and wills the concept as such, the form of the ought. Over against this, the [person] described previously is limited and constrained within this content X, which he does not cognize as a *particular* configuration [*Gestaltung*], image, and part of a higher whole, which is simply [*schlechthin*] hidden to his eyes. [He is] therefore incapable of cognizing or attending to anything toward which his enthusiasm is not directed. An indicator is that the moral [person] wills the whole law of duty, whereas the character being described wills only a part | of it, does not know that it is a part, but instead takes it to be something absolute, since the whole, and what is more, its form as a law, are hidden from his eyes.[7] Hence, (2) the moral [person] wills that the concept acquires its life. The life of the concept, however, is not merely his individual life but rather the life of all without exception [*schlechthin*]. He therefore wills completely the morality of all. Just as it belongs within the concept that it should take hold of all and make all into one single community, so too this belongs to his will, since his will is precisely that of the concept. Just as the concept works to take hold of all in an unconscious way, so the moral [person], as the conscious life of the concept, works in a conscious way. Articulated in a single plain phrase, this is the material character, the content of the moral will: the morality of all—obviously, just as long as this can still be an end, [i.e.,] in this life. The material [character]—we articulated the formal [aspect] earlier, willing duty for the sake of duty. But until the true moral law appears, the absolute duty *of all* can only be conceived as the moralization of all, the upbuilding [*Erbauung*] [of all] into one single moral community. This is the love that I

---

7. HALLE: This would provide us with the first CRITERION for the moral disposition [*Gesinnung*]. In the one there is no x, y, or z. This will is directed not toward this or that shape of dutifulness but rather toward the idea [*Idee*] of absolute unity (IV/6, 129).

mentioned previously. We will discuss it further, as well as the material character that has been established. This is the sole content of our further reflections, and the goal of [what has been said] up to this point is [just] to describe this [moral] character.

First of all, in order to continue characterizing the antithesis from this point, [we arrive at] the following. To the extent that the particular content | of the will = X is a state of human society, the moral [person] wills it by way of the morality of society and in absolutely no other way. [The members of society] should conceive of [this state] for themselves, and their wills should be purified to the point that they will it. This enlightenment and cultivation [*Aufklärung u. Bildung*] is, of course, his primary concern, and his will is that X should not be introduced in a different way. [The person,] however, who occupies the [previously] described standpoint wills X by any means, because it is absolute to him, and he will establish it with whatever means are in his power. He does not honor freedom, i.e., the clear, reflective [*besonnene*] life of the concept, because he does not possess it, and thus the vocation of his species for freedom remains hidden to him. The moral [person], however, comprehends his species only as something originally and essentially free; he cannot take anything else about it into account, since everything else is void [*nichtig*]. He intends what he does for it through his own reflective freedom, because it is only on this condition that it is obtained.[8]

---

8. HALLE: The moral person strives first for the development of reflective freedom; he wants to give form [*bilden*] only to a *morally* free community. This is the second CRITERION for distinguishing [the moral character] (IV/6, 129).

Lecture 22

(July 31, 1812)

II/13, 363　Overview.

The task {was} to fully describe the appearance of a moral will. To that end, we first needed a principle for the content of such a will. Now this has been discovered. First and foremost [*fürs erste*], the moral will wills the *morality of all* (this is sufficient for the present life; a different [prin-

StA 355　ciple] is not known within [the moral will]). This is its | only end [*Zwek*], the ultimate [end] of every possible end that [the moral will] can posit for itself.

Two criteria {were established}. One is *purely formal*. The moral will eternally wills the eternal, i.e., purely formal, concept, i.e., in abstraction from any configuration that it acquires in time. This form of the will negates the changing temporal form of the concept and exhibits it in its sublime unity beyond all time.

The second [criterion] is qualitatively formal. The moral will wills the morality of all in this eternal unity, [it] wills that all life within appearance becomes the life of the concept. This form of the will negates the division [*Spaltung*] of life into individual worlds, as the second fundamental division, and it exhibits the concept in its sublime unity beyond this multiplicity.[1]

Considered speculatively, the moral will is, therefore, the factually exhibited unity of absolute appearance that [itself] originally exists. God {is} one, [and] appearance {is}

---

1. HALLE: The two absolute grounds of multiplicity are infinite time and the world of the individual. The moral will transcends both (IV/6, 130).

[also] one beyond its appearing. In the moral will, [appearance] is once again one in its appearing. The moral will is thus the cessation [*Stillstand*] of every *fluctuating appearance* [*fliessenden Erscheinens*] to the extent that, as was recalled earlier, it provides a fixed standpoint to appearance. Appearance flows out of it according to its laws, while [the moral will] no longer flows or changes but stands unwaveringly beyond all time. The poet, with God in mind, says that if everything circulates in a continual flux, a serene spirit [*Geist*] abides in the flux.[2] One should not personify in this manner. The moral will is this serene spirit. There are, by the way, other predicates that are ascribed to God, including those that obtain of Him when he is thought of in the purest way, which are predicates of the moral will.

Before proceeding to the analysis, we want to dismiss some still unsatisfied demands of speculation; the theory of ethics has accomplished quite a bit for the whole system of philosophy, [something] which has also been touched on earlier [*einiges, das die Sittenlehre dem ganzen System der Philosophie zu leisten hat, das auch oben schon berührt ist*].

(1) The absolute concept, i.e., the true, qualitative content of appearance, the immediate, true, pure image of God, does not emerge in a collective consciousness [*GesamtBewußtseyn*], because there is no collective consciousness. Instead, it only emerges within individual consciousness! How, then, does this image within each individual consciousness relate to the one and only true image? Obviously it is an image of that image, and [the image] of each particular individual is distinguished from those of all the rest according to the law of the organic unity of a concept out of many [parts].[3] If all of these individual images

---

2. The editors indicate that the reference is to Schiller's 1797 "Die Worte des Glaubens." The relevant passage runs: "Und ein Gott ist, ein heiliger Wille lebt, / Wie auch der menschliche wanke; / Hoch über der Zeit und den Raume webt / Lebendig der höchste Gedanke. / Und ob alles in ewigen Wechsel kreist, / Es beharret im Wechsel ein ruhiger Geist." See *Schillers Sämtliche Werke, Erster Band* (Stuttgart: J. G. Cotta'sche Buchhandlung, 1879), 234–235.

3. HALLE: It must be an image of an image. Not *SCHEMA PRIMUM* but rather *SCHEMA SECUNDUM* [. . .] (IV/6, 130).

are conceived through one another, then their unity and their specific difference become clear on the basis of a single principle, and thus the true image that lies at the basis of all is comprehended. But [the latter] is first of all the true concept, which is supposed to obtain its life as a result of the moral will. To this end, it must, however, first obtain a consciousness. The form of such a consciousness is described this way: every individual, without exception, must become acquainted with the images of all the others and must comprehend his own [image] within an organic unity with those. Then all the rest would have the one true concept or image, which could now be transferred [*versetzen*] into life through a shared power.

(2) But how is it that, within each individual consciousness, this conditioned knowledge of the images of all [individuals] is supposed to attain to this unitary concept [*Einheitsbegriff*]? Only the individual image appears immediately within each [individual] (and considerable preparation is required even for this appearance). In so doing it does not yet thereby appear to others. For this to be achieved, it must not remain in an inert [*träger*], dead contemplation [*Betrachtung*] but rather {must} *be alive*, for only in that way does it enter into the sphere of appearance that is universally valid. That would be the first point.[4] The individual image appears first of all in a restricted temporal shape [*Zeitgestalt*], because it must appear for the first time at some particular time. Were all of life somehow swallowed up and possessed by this individual shape, it would not develop into its further configuration [*Gestaltung*]. It can only do so if the individual who contemplates it does not remain a blind instrument but rather elevates himself to willing the concept of duty in its mere form, thereby willing it in every shape in such a way that its progressive configuration unfolds in his life. {This can only happen} if he elevates himself to the moral disposition. That would be the second point.

---

4. CAUER: It follows from this that each [individual] must will that all the rest live a higher, spiritual [*geistiges*] life, so that he can come to know [the true image].

(3) Each [individual] wills, and must do so, just as certainly as the concept belongs within his willing, that the development of the true image of the unitary concept arise within him. This is only possible through the morality of all, which is one with his own; each [individual] must, henceforth and forever, will the morality of all.[5]

There is something else that belongs here, which is a not unimportant element of the philosophical theory of ethics and which we want to communicate. I said [previously that the moral person wills the] morality of *all* as of a completed [*geschloßenen*] system. The moral [person], therefore, must will that this system be completed [*sich schließe*], and he knows that it must be completed. Still, he also knows, equally well, that it cannot be completed until every individual image appears, or emerges into the life that is collectively [*gemeinsamen*] intuited, and is raised by all to the level of a unitary concept. Thus, he knows that this world, into whose series new individuals are continually entering in order to be formed [*zu ihrer Bildung*], this world of being born and passing away, must at some point come to an end, and that a world must come into being in which the species, now a completed unity, carries out its real business of actualizing the true image that has now appeared. The latter [world] is that for whose sake alone the present one exists, as a condition of its possibility. Moral consciousness is consciousness of the world in itself. This is the appearance of the *absolute* image.[6] The present, given [world] is not [the appearance of the absolute image] and can never be it, for the image cannot appear within it, only the always imperfect image of the image. But how might it be? [This world] is, like all lower stages, the visibility and condition of the possibility of the true world in itself, and it is only able to exist to the extent that this lies at its basis. Moral cognition therefore regards the present life as something temporary [*gegenwärtig*] and provisional and is certain of

---

5. There is a break indicated in Fichte's manuscript at this point.
6. HALLE: This is the appearance of schema I. If this obtains life at some point, and appearance becomes nothing other than the development of schema I in the unanimity [*Einmüthigkeit*] of all, then the true world has begun (IV/6, 131).

a future [life] and of the mutual bond between both. What is said about this relation on the basis of other sources can be combined with and corrected by this view. The *formally* moral will, which simply wills *duty*, is continually possible, and it exists eternally in this shape. But the law itself, in its content, should first be ascertained through this life. Elsewhere: worlds beyond worlds, and infinite series. This is still true, and has a different principle that does not belong [in the present discussion].[7, 8, 9]

---

7. Fichte is apparently referring to a discussion of Kant's remarks on multiple worlds in his own *Facts of Consciousness* lectures of 1810–1811 (II/12, 128).

8. CAUER: Whoever has the right moral will has eternal life, and to that extent there is no opposition [between the present life and the future life]. But the situation is different with respect to the law insofar as its *content* is concerned. In this respect there are two fundamental lives [*Grundleben*], a life of preparation and a true life. It is said that there must be a life that infinitely develops, and this is correct. But this claim is based upon objective appearance. For the sake of the world, and because a community of minds acts efficaciously upon the world, individual tasks must exist in the [future] world.

9. HALLE: The division into two lives is wrong; instead, there must be infinite systems of life [*Lebenssysteme*]. This is not based purely on the moral concept. There are, nevertheless, two worlds that differ completely in their character (IV/6, 132).

Lecture 23

(August 4, 1812)

StA 359   To return to the context [*Zusammenhang*]: (1) {The} absolutely *formal morality*, that of an individual I, insofar as there is no immediately self-conscious life apart from this form, consists in the absorption [*Aufgehen*] and disappearance of its own life into the life of the concept. This does not {occur} within time but rather as a *unity of life* and thus through the absolute will.

The concept that is supposed to be alive here is assumed in this instance to be simply unknown [*schlechthin unbekannte*], [something] not investigated by thought *a priori*, but rather [something] absolutely given to the con-

II/13, 366   sciousness that is directed toward it. *Attend* to yourself. |

With that, the theory of ethics would be finished. Such a theory would also suffice for practice [*für das praktische*]. Nothing is to be added to this principle [*Satze*]. {This would be} the first part {of the theory of ethics}: the pure theory of ethics.[1]

---

1. CAUER: In the absolute form of morality, the concept is assumed as unknown—as something that will emerge within a consciousness that is dedicated to it. For practical purposes, it is sufficient to say [to someone that you should] follow the voice of your conscience. If there were nothing further [to say], the theory of ethics would be finished. This would be the *pure* part of the theory of ethics. But a further question has yet to be raised: can nothing more precise be said about the content of the concept? Can it not be defined in its universal form so that what the voice of conscience says would be grasped in its universal character? This would be the second, applied, part of the theory of ethics.

(2) Second question [*sic*]: can the content of this concept not be determined in its general form, in an image formed according to the laws of the concept, with respect to its character? {This would be} the second part [of the theory of ethics]: the applied theory of ethics. {Its} goal [*Zwek*] {would be} to bring forth an explicit [*äussere*] theory of ethics that holds universally, which already assumes a multitude [*Mehrheit*] of individuals and a commonality [*Gemeinschaftlichkeit*] of cognition. {This would be} an external criterion that is objectively valid. |

By means of a thorough investigation, {the claim about the concept put forth at the beginning of the lectures} has fallen apart into a duality [*Duplicität*]. For the *true world*, which does not {yet} exist but which ought to come into being, {the concept consists in} bringing forth a certain objective world, that of the divine image, within objective being. For the *present* world {it consists in} bringing forth morality, i.e., the absolute good will, *within the entire species*, which is a condition of its goal of an objective creation of the world. If we take it seriously, {our} immediate {concern} is never an *objective* being but rather only the willing of *something different. Being* only exists there {in the true world}; here, [in the present world,] the concept requires a will outside of itself. The absolute, final goal of the moral will here below {is} *a morality outside of itself*. The object of a human being is always [another] human being.[2] (I do not know whether this has ever been clearly articulated in the theory of ethics. [This is] a doctrine that we will be called upon to remember often enough as we go forward; it clearly demonstrates the spirit [*Geist*] of this [theory of ethics]. In this way the theory of ethics has obtained uncommon clarity and simplicity.)

From now on, we are only concerned with the analysis of this proposition.

---

2. HALLE: If we are completely serious, the moral law never demands a being in this world but rather always only a moral will outside of itself. The true object of the truly moral human being is always the human being himself. Here there is nothing else for the moral law (IV/6, 132).

First of all, {I want} to prefix a remark that holds good for the whole [discussion]. We are [asserting something] in this proposition on the basis of the *freely conceived character* of the concept in the present world. (a) If we are right about this, then the concept that in fact appears and takes hold of the moral life must be accompanied by this character, though without any assistance on the part of freedom or consciousness. Our opinion must therefore be that nothing else is ever commanded in this life through the absolute concept of duty than what relates to morality outside of us and | has this as its goal. The actions of someone who actually follows the voice of his conscience according to the formal concept of morality as such always have this as their goal, whether or not [this person] knows it. The concept that has been presented is a matter of scientific clarity. It is good and useful that a human being be completely clear, because he can then promote his aims [*Zweke*] with others more easily; but this is not unconditionally [*schlechthin*] part of the form of the moral will. Someone can therefore | be moral who acts in this spirit [*Geiste*] without himself knowing it; {there can be someone} who acts to promote morality outside of himself unconsciously. Such a person still promotes [this goal], and should someone [try to] explain his action, it cannot be done otherwise than on the basis of this goal.[3]

StA 361

II/13, 367

This is the place to incorporate this [point] into a deeper context. The entire present world has no other purpose [*Absicht*] for its existence than the formation [*Bildung*] of humanity for morality. Everything that comes to pass through the obscure and unconscious appearance of the *concept*, the very same one that is the ground of the world and the cause of world's development [*WeltEntwikler*], aims at this goal [*Zwek*]. Its aim is, of course, only *this free* and

---

3. HALLE: The concept set forth here [*aufgestellte*] belongs to scientific clarity, and that is important, but it does not entirely belong to the form of moral willing itself. Only that one obeys [the law] belongs to [the latter]. Someone can act in the true spirit of morality without knowing this spirit (IV/6, 133).

conscious morality; [the goal] is not that people be made moral against their wills or without their awareness. Any efficacious action [aimed at the latter state of affairs] would be immoral, contrary to morality [*widersittlich*]. [The point is rather that the concept] can and should employ human beings for reflection [*Besinnung*] and the bringing forth of the good will. The world is, at each moment, the best, not indeed with respect to happiness or enjoyment but rather with respect to the moral formation [*Bildung*] of all. [The world] is the first, immediately and factually given means for the appearance of the divine image, insofar as it forms the human species into a second means or instrument for this appearance. This is simply what it is, through the inner necessity of its | being within the divine, and it cannot be otherwise. To this extent, one is entirely within one's rights to speak of a governance of the world, a providence, so long as one does not think in an anthropomorphic manner that God {acts} in time, [recognizing] instead that He acts outside of and beyond all time, through His appearing within the world.

{I said} the present world; but the will of the moral [person] is the same as [the purpose of the] world, and the same concept [determines both], though it has broken through to a clear consciousness that guides life [in the case of the moral person]. [The moral person's will] therefore cannot contain anything else but what the [purpose of the] world also contains, [namely,] the morality of all. That which belongs obscurely within the occurrence of the world and depends upon reflection and contemplation belongs clearly within the way of life [*Wandel*] of the moral person and is as apparent to the reflection and contemplation of all as it is to him, since no mechanical compulsion should take place. The way of life of each [individual] ought always to be edifying for others, whether he wills it or not, because it cannot be otherwise and is this way according to an intelligible [*geistigen*] law. Simply through living in this manner, each provides a witness to everyone with whom he comes into contact that a life carried out dutifully

II/13, 368 is possible, whether or not he intends [to give this witness].[4, 5, 6]

Once again, in this life, whether it is aware of it or not, the moral will constantly has a morality outside of itself as its goal. This goal is not somehow contingent or merely ancillary but rather is essential and is a sure external criterion. You say that what you are doing is commanded of you. We cannot separate your immediate self-consciousness from the manifestations that you thereby acquire. However, as a consequence of universal lawfulness [*Gesezmässigkeit*], we know the sphere in which these must be contained. If, for

StA 363 example, you say | that it is commanded of you by your conscience that nations [*Völker*] be exterminated as a punishment for their sins, or that they be forced with fire and sword to adopt a certain confession or constitution, then we can say with confidence that you are deceiving yourself, for the free, moral power can never command such things. Of course, you could be so commanded as a mere force of nature in the way that a flame or a hurricane could also be commanded to destroy, since nothing exists without the command of the world's divine governance. We ought to employ appearances caused by [natural forces] just as much as those caused by you for the purposes of our vocation,

---

4. CAUER: This is the *unfree* development of the image of God. The moral will is the same as and necessarily contains what the world also contains—the moral formation [*Bildung*] *of all*—but it is expressed in the way of life of the moral human being *clearly* and *consciously*.

5. HALLE: This is the *unfree* development of the image of God. The moral law is identical [in both cases], only it has broken through into clear consciousness [in the case of the moral person]. Thus the moral will cannot contain anything but what the world contains = the moral formation *of all*—but it is expressed *clearly* and *consciously* in the way of life of a human being. The world expresses our moral vocation in an obscure way. The way of life of each [individual] ought to be continually edifying for others. And, if it is moral, it is incapable of anything else, whether one intends this or not (IV/6, 133).

6. Fichte's manuscript indicates a break at this point. It is notable that the material on violence that follows in the manuscript is missing from both extant transcripts.

but you occupy a status that is no different from that of these natural forces, not a moral [status]. The [present] age itself makes it necessary to recall and emphasize this point. One hears people who claim to believe that, since violent destruction is now the order of the day and belongs to the plan of the world's divine governance (something that is merely their opinion and cannot be proven), it is their duty to join in the destruction. Someone who has no knowledge of duty can be so perverted that he carries out his plan in a violent manner; but whoever has such knowledge acts against his own conscience if he goes along with such a plan. A human being ought never to participate in the governance of the world, for he ought never to become a *world*; he leaves this to God. Instead, he ought to elevate himself to the sphere of freedom and reflection [*Besonnenheit*], where he has a different end. This is even more true given that the violent deeds of human beings are never directly part of the divine governance of the world, for human beings collectively are called [*bestimmt*] to freedom and reflection, and [violent deeds] occur simply through the guilt of the human beings who perpetrate them. Of course, [violent deeds] could become | a means for the improvement of others according to the very same divine plan of the world.[7] |

The moral will. We need to describe (1) the prevailing and constant disposition that results from it: the inner appearance of the mind [*Gemüth*]. {We have to} (2) accompany it through the different domains of action and become familiar with its manner of action in these.

{I will begin with} the description of the inner disposition; namely, the fixed [disposition] that [it] does not produce itself but that *exists* within it, because it is itself the result of something else, i.e., of its morality as such. {This is at the same time} the description of the appearance that [the moral person] must always have for himself, in case he intuits himself.[8]

---

7. Fichte's manuscript indicates a break at this point.

8. CAUER: First of all, we need to describe the inner appearance of the *mind* of a moral person. (2) We must also consider his *actions*. In this way, we will deliver what we have promised—a theory of the appearance [*Erscheinungslehre*] of a moral person.

Lecture 24

(August 5, 1812)

(1) Selflessness [*Selbstlosigkeit*]. Self-*denial* [*Selbst*verläugnung] says too little, pointing to an act [. . .] becoming.¹ There is no {self-denial}, since [*the moral person*] *has no self*.

(It is proof of the fact that the vulgar person understands nothing of the higher [person] and has an antagonistic attitude toward the latter that, among other things, there is the frequent assurance in theories about God and ethics that it is quite impossible and contrary to nature to forget and abandon oneself, | and that [therefore] these could not be commanded.² We say, on the contrary, that it is the most natural, the easiest, the simplest thing of all. For me it is far easier to comprehend what is not myself than [to comprehend] myself. Doing the latter is already a complex manner of thinking that has undergone a transformation.)

That this is the case has been shown already and follows [from what has been said] as a consequence. The I

---

1. The ellipses indicate illegible words in Fichte's manuscript.

2. [Fichte's marginal note:] This is an absolute lack of vision [*NichtSehen*], being closed off [*Verschlossenheit*], and a deficiency of vision based on greed. Should one ask [people who hold this view] what depends on their existing or not, they will never have an intelligible response. They will offer nothing but "I *will* that I exist, and I cannot abandon this willing." They could be correct to the extent that they posit their factual condition [*Zustand*] as absolute. But here I recall a remark that I have already made on another occasion and that one needs to repeat throughout [the discussion of] this material: How do they, as individuals, arrive at an ideal, [how do they] form a basic image [*Grundbilde*] of the human species so that they [can] assume that none may be better than or greater than them?

is a substantial thing in itself [*Ding an sich*] that, once again, has its accidents, results, requirements, etc. [It is a] life principle that wills to preserve itself. As a result of the moral will, this private [*eigene*] life has been elevated to [the life of] the *concept*, of the command of duty, which lives in place of the apparent I *within this life that is copied* [*abgebildetes*]. The I is nothing more than the occurrence of an image within the sphere of actuality; yet, I were no life being copied here, then no life would exist in this place, nothing would be stirring, rather it would be dead. This is because, for itself and without the life prefigured [*vorgebildetes*] in concepts, it is completely unable to initiate an actual state [*Zustand*]. |

Grasp this precisely. {The I is} *the principle of an actuality*, either through itself (admittedly, only in the immoral appearance) {or} unconditionally [*schlechthin*] *not through itself*, but rather through the image that lies within the concept. In the latter manner, [the I] is not at all a self, and there is no feeling [of self], nor love [of self], or of anything at all, which would have to be put to death.[3]

(That there are, in fact, no individuals, but rather that these are merely forms of self-appearance that result from the formal laws of self-appearance, is a theoretical proposition of the [*Wissenschaftslehre*]. Since the beginning of the world, every wise and good person has proclaimed this proposition practically through their own being.)

Thus, by means of breaking through, the concept creates itself and attains its own life, completely by itself. The I founders; it does not somehow annihilate itself through freedom but rather is annihilated. It loses its feeling and idea of itself because another idea fills the mind and takes possession of it, a fact that is immediately evident on the

---

3. CAUER: Nothing comes between the individual command and its fulfillment. There is no thinking it over and [then] making a decision; that which comes between would be the I. [Viewed] from another side, the I is always a principle of itself—either *through itself* (admittedly, only in appearance)—in which case it is the immoral I—or it is a principle of itself through the image in a concept that comes between—it is a real likeness [*Abbild*] of the ideal image in a concept—here, the I vanishes completely.

basis of our assumption. This is why I said that this selflessness is the easiest thing of all, since it comes to be as a mere occurrence without any assistance from freedom. It is also the clearest thing of all, since it immediately follows from our basic concept.

[Now] to consider the individual, though not with respect to how he wills his own morality and becomes an object to himself of thought and of willing, of his own treatment [*Bearbeitung*]: I's outside of him do become such objects for him, but only to the extent that they are conceived of as immoral, and to that extent as having a self [that needs to be] *cultivated* [*gebildet*] for morality (that is, the self should be extirpated from their [the I's] place within the collective appearance). [The individual is also not being considered] with respect to {the fact that he can will his own morality}, since the assumption is that he is [already] moral and is aware of his absolute will to unconditionally obey the voice of duty. | A human being cannot somehow make himself moral through willing to be so, as was already demonstrated. Such a will, provided of course that it actually is a *will*, a dedication and a task of the entire I in this resolve, would itself already be morality. Perhaps [in some case] there is no *will* but rather merely a wish, a yearning, as a result of which one would gladly do what is right and perhaps find himself in the condition that we love and esteem, but *only* if he did *not* have to give up this or that, or do this or that, being unable to decide; such a person is not moral, his self depends upon these [supposedly] exempted things that he cannot resolve to sacrifice, though he is on | the path toward morality.[4] He has already attained something great beyond

---

4. [Original:] Ist es vielleicht kein *Wille*, sondern nur ein Wunsch, u. Sehnen; zufolge dessen man gern recht thun, u. in diesem vielleicht von uns geliebten, u. geschätzen Zustande sich befinden möchte, wenn *nur nicht* dann das u. das unterlassen werden sollte, und das gethan, wozu wir uns nicht entschließen können, so ist ein solcher Mensch nicht sittlich, sein Selbst hängt eben an diesen vorbehaltnen Dingen, zu deren Opfer er sich nicht entschließen kann: obwohl er auf dem Wege der Sittlichkeit ist [. . .].

[the former] person if only the longing for morality has awakened in him.⁵

I say that the moral [person] is no longer an object to himself at all; such a point of disconnection between [will and] appearance is completely removed from his sight. *Is*—that is where the accent lies. The *natural* self, and the love of it in which he was born, have completely vanished by means of the morality within him. In this sense the proposition holds without exception.

Should [the moral person] nevertheless once more become an object of thought, of willing, of treatment, this could only come about through the *command of duty* itself; and, since in this command, [the moral person,] like every other individual, is regarded only as an *instrument* and as a means, this could only come about through a particular command that obtains for a time and brings with it its own cessation. | He could be assigned the task of bringing forth something within himself so that, once it is finished, he might use it; thus, [only] for a time [*drum auf Zeit*]; but this directedness toward himself can never again be brought forth as an enduring state, since [the self] is completely annihilated.

This [scenario] could occur in the following cases. (a) The command of duty might not be *clear* to him; only an obscure representation might arise in him of what ought to occur through him at the place that he occupies. Of course, in that case, he should not act at all in accord with this obscure representation. He should cease to act and [should] pause. But he ought to work on himself [in order

---

5. CAUER: The I of the moral person does not even become an object in the sense of willing his own morality [*Nicht einmal in der Rücksicht daß er seine Sittlichkeit wolle wird dem Sittlichen sein Ich zum Objekt*]. I's outside of him become objects that he deals with, but only to the extent that their selves, their immorality, should be annihilated. A human being cannot make himself moral through willing to be moral, for this will, in its truth, would already be morality. It could be the case that such a will is called so incorrectly, that it is merely a wish or a yearning for morality—one would gladly be moral if only one did not have to give up this or that, or do this or that. This demonstrates that it is not a will at all. Such a person may well find himself on the path toward morality—one has already achieved a lot by merely bringing a human being to the point of love and admiration for morality.

to achieve] a clear understanding of it, in which case he will most certainly succeed if there is indeed actually a command of duty within this obscure concept. A few comments on this that should not be passed over in a theory of ethics: [namely, that] a representation is obscure as long as a determinate action *that is thoroughly possible* [*durchaus möglich*] by every means is not expressed by it. In this case, the concept has not been developed into a living image. The moral will, however, is merely the realization of such images, hence it is obvious that the moral [person] does not act in accord with such representations but rather pauses, remaining inert and motionless. Elevating the concept from this obscure condition into clarity is a private affair [*eigne Sache*]. It is the business of the moral I [*des sittlichen Ich Sache ist*] to be dedicated to it, to attend to it, and this attention appears as deliberation and inquiry [*Nachdenken u. Erforschen*]. [. . .].[6, 7, 8] He does not act; *quod dubitas, ne feceris* {is} a principle that is entirely correct.[9] It is quite wrong to claim to have acted on the basis of an *erring* conscience. [The conscience] never errs, though what it utters can be obscure. In that case, *do not act*. Indeed, conscience forbids you to act. Whoever nonetheless does act occupies the previously I described stage of the individual will, I which can, as far as its content goes, be [a stage of] vision; he does not [occupy] the moral [stage] at all. If he talks about conscience, he is deceiving himself and is acting on the basis of willful drives, not on the basis of obedience [to the moral law]. (All religious persecutions that one thinks of as being cast in a favorable light by means of this excuse belong to this sphere.) One says: [What] if I must act now,

---

6. [Original:] Hier wird durch den Begriff selbst der sittliche spekulirend u. betrachtend: was er an sich nicht ist: auch nicht etwa auf den Vorrath, was er auch nie ist, sondern durch das gegenwärtige Gesez aufgefodert.

7. CAUER: Enjoined [to do so] by the present law, the moral person will speculate till reaching the point of clarity.

8. HALLE: In this way the moral person will speculate, not act; he does not act before the law is clear to him (IV/6, 136).

9. Latin: "Do not do that of which you are in doubt." The phrase originates with Pliny the Younger, *Epistulae* I, 18, 5.

on the spot? I see only one situation in which one would have to do so, namely, that of a civic office [*bürgerlichen Amte*]. Here one has the guidance of the law, and it is always right to proceed in accordance with [law]; in case there is no [law], then one must make inquiries. In his time it comes down to the highest legislator [*Wohl, da kommt es zu seiner Zeit an den höchsten Gesezgeber*]. He has time to consider [the matter] for himself. Aside from this circumstance, one should not and must not act on the spot. Only something arbitrary could commit us to doing so.[10]

Or, (b) the law is indeed clear, but the individual does not have the power or the means to put it into action. In that case, it is enjoined upon him as an intermediate command to acquire this power and these means. He now takes himself immediately to be the object of his labor and of his thought, though not as himself or for his own sake, nor for the sake of some state of being of himself nor for pleasure but rather as the instrument of the task that has arisen for him.

Or, (c) the physical self-preservation of the person, as the universally recognized vehicle for all moral legislation in this place within the context of appearance, might be endangered. In that case the immediate command is to secure this for the sake of all the other commands that are issued or could be issued to him. [This is] not so that this person will be secured, on which nothing as such depends, but rather so that the realization of the commands that have been enjoined upon this person will be secured. The human being ought to preserve himself as an instrument of the moral law, since the moral person does not consider himself to be anything but this. |

[Physical self-preservation must be secured] for the sake of morality and thus within the sphere of means that are moral and just. It does not matter that so and so as such exists, but rather that morality, which assumes the form of

---

10. CAUER: That someone would have to act *then and there* [*auf der Stelle*] could only occur in a civic office, where one must always act according to the established law; or, if there is none, one must inquire after it, and the highest authority [*Behörde*] can reflect on it.

justice [*Gerechtigkeit*] when it is a question of the conflict between the coexistence of several individuals, be asserted. If this goal [*Zwek*] [of self-preservation] cannot be achieved through *just* means, then the moral law clearly rescinds the existence of this person, which, therefore, should not be asserted but rather relinquished [*aufgegeben werden*]. The physical and moral worlds are the representational [*bildliche*] expression of the same basic concept, only in a double form, and the moral order holds equally for the moral will as for the [physical world]. That which perishes through the moral world order, | i.e., that which must perish for the preservation of the moral world order, can be preserved just as little as that which perishes through the physical world order. For example, one person dies because of illness, and another dies because of the preservation of justice. Both [take place] according to God's will; the former, according to [a will that is] incomprehensible, the latter according [to a will that] is quite clear and comprehensible. This claim holds universally, both for us and for others, and I want to advance it directly here. Just as my preservation [is commanded] for me, so is that of everyone else. They ought to exist for the same reason [as I do, namely,] for the {preservation} of an instrument of the moral law. I may not, however, {preserve} myself or anyone else by unjust means.

Lecture 25

(August 6, 1812)

(2) Love, universal philanthropy [*Menschenliebe*].[1] One loves that in relation to which and for the sake of which one wills everything that one wills: the constant, permanent, basic object [*GrundObjekt*] of our will, that which all of our thinking and willing ever keep before our eyes. For the immoral [person], this [basic object] is | his I; for the moral [person], it is humanity as a whole [*die gesamte Menschheit*], and in particular those members of it with whom he enters into a relationship, on whose behalf he has already acted and brought something about [*gewirkt*], who are encompassed by his definite plans, i.e., the neighbor [*der Nächste*], to use the biblical expression, which is quite apt. This is how it must be, for [the moral person] wills morality and, by that means, the blessedness [*Seeligkeit*] of all.

(1) Therefore, [the moral person] does not isolate [*sondert*] himself but rather remains in a reciprocal relationship with human beings to the extent that the business that is assigned to him by the command of duty allows. It follows that his constant, i.e., indeterminate, will, would be to stand in the closest [possible] connection with as many [people] as possible. Someone might say, "I only want to keep myself pure and unsullied, to care for myself and for my morality alone. What responsibility do I have for others?" [This] is in total conflict with the moral disposition

---

1. HALLE: A second basic characteristic [*Grundzug*] of the moral mind [*Gemüthes*] is love, universal philanthropy (IV/6, 137).

[*Gesinnung*]. By "morality" such a person can only mean a merely external and negative avoidance of evil, an external civil [*bürgerliche*] justice and respectability.[2] This is not morality, and it is the gravest of errors to deceive oneself in this way and to believe that one has thereby satisfied the requirement. {This is} Pharisaism. True morality consists in love and in action alone; therefore, whoever loves duty, whose entire mind [*Gemüth*] is filled by willing it, thereby also loves communion [*Gemeinschaft*] with human beings, which this duty requires of him.[3]

This is the universal affection [*Neigung*] that occupies his mind; sincere agreement [*innige Verständigung*] with his species as far as can be extended, through a constant openness | for new connections. The connections that he actually has | possess a determinate purpose, for here he is subject to the command that, just as arbitrariness ought not to enter into his whole life, so should there be nothing at all in his relationships without purpose. An idle concern with stockpiling and taking on relationships cannot be part of his action. For this reason, a truly moral [person] could also separate himself for a time in order to first work on himself and cultivate [*bilden*] himself for the effect that he intends (according to the comment made yesterday). He {does this} out of love, in order thereby to be able to act with that much more benevolence [*wohlthätiger*]. One accuses, for example, [some] studies, particularly those deep ones that are distant from the vulgar understanding, of making people unhappy. As far as it goes with respect to what is commonly called happiness, i.e., aimless worry about, among other things, enjoying oneself while bored in social gatherings, it would be no serious reproach to these studies that they cure one of this [worry]. However, all scientific efforts must, without exception, be subordinated to the fundamental goal of

---

2. CAUER: Morality is not negative—do nothing evil.

3. HALLE: Negative purity [*Reinigkeit*], not morality, is expressed by self-purification [*Sichselbstreinigung*]. [The latter] is genuine Pharisaism. Morality is not the absence of external civil criminality [*Unsträflichkeit*]; instead, it is concerned with others' lives. No one can be moral for himself alone, since here the INDIVIDUAL is nothing and only the community [exists] (IV/6, 137).

earthly life, to the formation [*zu bilden*] of the community for morality, which is in any case a social goal. Now it may be true of these studies that those who dedicate themselves to them through their inner law must at first withdraw into themselves for a while in order to acquire within themselves the power to have an effect on the whole. In that case, withdrawal is merely a means for a properly efficacious sociability [*kräftiges Geselligkeit*] and leads to it, so that this is entirely within the bounds set by our rule.⁴

(3) Humanity as a whole is embraced by {the moral person} and is dear to his heart [*ist an sein liebender Herz gelegt*] as the instrument of morality and not in any other regard. All other love and affection are pathological, are not moral but rather are in some sense natural, i.e., based on something incomprehensible.⁵ Therefore they always give way to and subordinate themselves to the higher moral love, notwithstanding the fact that they can remain within the obscure depths of nature; we will find an application for them.

(a) All {human beings} without exception {are dear to the heart of the moral person}; they are given to him this way in his moral cognition, and he cannot give up this opinion without giving up morality itself. He therefore does not give up on anyone who bears a human visage, however he might seem. Just as long as nature tolerates someone in life, which is, after all, the expression of the concept, [the moral person] also tolerates him and *has faith* and *hope*. It is just as certain as the fact that this person is alive that the concept, or God, wills that he improve himself and pre-

---

4. HALLE: The moral [person] wills to mingle with people as intimately and as widely as possible. His actual connections, however, always have a definite purpose. Caprice [*Willkühr*] has no place in his life. He satisfies a certain inclination and yet keeps his mind open for every connection that is demanded by the moral law. Thus, a truly moral person can separate [*absondern*] himself for a while in order to render himself an efficient instrument of action. Even this separation occurs for the sake of the species—out of a deep love (IV/6, 137).

5. HALLE: Every other love and affection is pathological, [i.e.,] not moral; it may well be natural, i.e., based upon some incomprehensible, i.e., natural, relationships (IV/6, 137).

supposes [that he will do so]. [The moral person] does not believe or will in any other way than the concept does, and so he also believes and wills [that the other will improve himself]. Judgment and condemnation are as far from him as they are from the absolute concept. |

(b) The *moral foundation* [*Grundlage*] within human beings, and its development, are the *only* basis for his love. [The moral person] therefore does not love *what is evil* in someone, nor does he tolerate or excuse it without regard to the person, whatever his natural affection may say, since the latter is entirely subordinated to the higher love. As a result of his will, this affection ought to disappear wherever it is found, precisely because he loves the person that truly endures, the moral germ [*Keim*], and wants to free [that germ] from its husk [*Umhüllung*]. But it should disappear through proper means, through knowledge and love of what is better, not through compulsion or deceit. He wants to have the person freely, not to make him the slave of fear or of some error.

(c) This alone is the basis of his love. The one who is internally perfect and self-sufficient in doing what is right through his absolute will is externally needy and dependent upon the entire human species. He is needy of their moral cultivation [*Bildung*]; the absence of it grieves him deeply, while its appearance delights him as something that satisfies his deepest need. Yet, he is only dependent in this [one] respect; the whole human species can neither give nor take anything from him and there is nothing in the world that could bring him either joy or distress. He wants a dynamic [*kräftiges*] *life* and *to have an effect*! Undoubtedly so, | but only within the moral order and through the means that exist along with it. If his efficacy is inhibited, what about that can harm him? Is he somehow an egotist who dreams of and seeks after his own merit [*Verdienst*], who wants to do everything himself only so that he has himself done it? O, how far would he be then from the true life! Did he want to accomplish something through immoral means, contending against the morality of others, disregarding their freedom? In that case he would have been immoral, and should the right disposition now awaken within him, he would have to rejoice deeply that [his action] was prevented. If, as we have assumed, he wills to have an effect through moral means, then his efficacy could only be prevented by the immorality of others, and this would certainly be a cause of pain for him since it is immorality.

(d) In this sense, and within these bounds of moral action, he is ever ready and driven to serve all. [He is] first and foremost [driven to serve] the preservation of each [person] for the very same reason, and within the same boundaries, as he [is driven to serve] his own. [He is driven to serve] the physical well-being of all, the existence of order in their surroundings, the legality of their constitution, and their freedom, in the way that we have defined these concepts in the theory of right [*RechtsLehre*]. He knows that it is only in these circumstances that they can lift their gaze to what is spiritual [*geistige*] and higher, and that external compulsion as a rule and according to the common standard takes everything higher about a person and forces it down nearly to the level of an animal.[6] {He is driven to serve all} for their instruction, inspiration, and elevation, and his powerful [*kräftige*] good will is the best teacher for each person; it provides insight and power that one may not have often sought for oneself and that cannot be accounted for on the basis of what has occurred hitherto. |

(e) [The moral person] does all of this not in a random manner and does not aim at salvation, beatitude, and conversion as if at some adventure—he does not seek out occasions idly, for the truly moral way of life is never idle—but rather as the plan of our lives and the unsought for relationships into which we enter bring along with them.[7]

---

6. [Original:] Denn er weiß, daß nur in einer solchen Lage sie ihren Blik erheben können auf das geistige, u. höhere, u. daß äußere Druk in der Regel u. nach dem gemeinen Maasstabe dem Menschen fast alles sein höheres nimmt, u. ihn beinahe zum Thier hernieder drükt.

7. HALLE: But [the moral person] will do all of this not in a disorderly way, without measure, goal, or purpose. He is not concerned about the instruction or conversion of others as some adventure; a truly moral course of life has no time for searching about. Here, there is not an individual appearance of morality but rather the eternal life of the concept. He is occupied at every moment (IV/6, 138).

(f) Indeed, {he does} all of this with the love previously described, with a deep, individual, heartfelt need [*Herzens-Bedürfniß*] for a moral state of affairs outside of us; only this love, this desire, this overflowing [*Ausfüllung*] of the heart is the seal [*Siegel*] of our morality. Someone could fulfill all of this and bring about more in external appearance than someone [else who is] truly gripped by the spiritual [*geistigen*] life, but it would avail him naught and would mean nothing for him, because he would not have love.[8]

---

8. Cf. 1 Corinthians 13:1–3.

Lecture 26

(August 7, 1812)

(3) Truthfulness and openness. [The moral person] is, first and foremost, *truthful* to himself. We assume [that he possesses] the absolute [moral] will, otherwise he would not be the appearance that we are describing. He immediately knows that he possesses it and is satisfied by this. As long as his life continues, no self arises for him. The development of a life from it can be brought to a halt, either through the obscurity of the command or from a lack of subjective power. Would he be able to conceal either from himself? To take *himself* to be *clear* [*klar*] or *able* [*kräftig*] [when he is not]? Why? The deficiency is not his affair but rather a matter of the *concept*, which does not now, in this particular circumstance, determine him as its instrument. | He is always obedient to it; he wills and loves what it loves, even including its obscurity and his own weakness, which are certainly part of the plan. What about this is supposed to cause him grief? Is it the loss of either his own or others' high opinion of himself, as an [. . .] instrument?[1] This is quite distant from his own perspective, according to which he does not exist either as someone worthy or unworthy; instead [he is] nothing. He is in himself entirely clear and transparent [*durchsichtig*] to himself [down] to the very root of his life. He either knows or doesn't know that the concept has said *what* it has said—in the former case, he knows that he would have to behave in a certain way; in the latter case, he knows that he does not know. [There is] no

---

1. Fichte's manuscript contains several illegible words.

obscure place that obstructs the light [*Anstoß des Lichts*] in this whole series.

Just as he is clear with himself regarding all his drives and the means [for realizing them], so he may also be [open] with anyone who desires [him to be so]; [he is] always ready to allow anyone access to what is within him, without reservation or hiding place, [so that they] see into the depths | just as he sees himself. Why should he not be? Whoever hides from himself wants *to deceive*. If others knew his true intentions and motives, he would not bring them around to his intentions [*so würde er sie nicht zu seinen Absichten bringen*]. That is something [the moral person] will never do, for, on account of this clear insight, he will never bring others around to calling something good when he himself does not have the insight [that it is so]. Whoever hides for a moral reason [*aus Sittlichkeit*] could only do so because the sight of what is within him would anger others and tempt them. {This} is not the situation [of the moral person]. The sight of what is within him can only *edify* [*erbauen*], and thus he would have to wish that everyone could see into what is within him and [that everyone] might look within him without hindrance. [A remark made] in passing, and in the interests of [articulating] the antithesis: the immoral, impure [person] does well to hide himself, since the sight of him would only anger and tempt [others]. If he has not brought [himself around] to inner purity of heart, | that is bad; still, he has not yet committed the serious evil of infecting or tempting anyone, nor has he made himself into a devil. He spares the sanctified community [*der sich heiligenden Gemeine*] the sight of what is within him and does not exacerbate inner immorality by exhibiting it shamelessly. He becomes a hypocrite! It is his responsibility if he becomes one, though it is not necessary [that he does so]. This only happens if he once again has the intention of infecting others, of controlling them for his own advantage; [it does] not [happen] if [this hiding] comes from the pure intention not to *anger* them. In the latter case he knows by that act that he does not approve of his own condition, does not think that it would be a good thing if everyone were that way; this can become for him a step on the road of actual improvement. Confessions of inner sinfulness previously touched upon, in which one presumptuously includes the human species [as a whole], are certainly offensive [*ärglich*] and corrupting to the highest degree. Admittedly, they come from the prejudice that one is giving honor to God, as well as of one's own humility, but they constitute a misunderstanding, one that is quite unhealthy and that one must work to extirpate.[2]

The origin of all doctrines about the duty of formal truthfulness lies in our statement that "you *absolutely* ought *not* to lie"; this has a deeper basis than one commonly believes. For us [this statement] means that the moral person necessarily, i.e., just as surely as he is [a moral person], always entirely lays open what is within him; [he is] absolutely [*schlechthin*] open and transparent, [presenting himself] just as he is according to his nature. The moral [person] never lies; no knowing falsehood belongs to the course of a moral life. We are not discussing what the immoral [person] does; this is not being posited; what matters is not an external appearance but rather morality itself. The state, however, in that it must achieve its goal without assuming universal morality (of which it | must become the chief means), and given that absolutely no one should tell it an untruth, must think of other available means for promoting truthfulness | among its citizens without a genuine moral foundation. We will not discuss this here.[3]

---

2. HALLE: If his life does not develop on the basis of the concept, this is not something he could conceal from himself, nor could he take himself to be *clear* when he is not; even less so could he deny his lack of power. This is indeed not his affair but rather that of the concept. What the concept lacks in clarity and power is not his affair. The good will alone is required, and he possesses this *ex hypothesi*. Thus, the moral [person] is clear and transparent to himself down to the root. That the concept says something to him, as well as what it says, are completely clear to him. An offense [*Anstoß*] or doubt are nowhere to be found; should one occur, he recognizes it clearly and is calm about it in that he awaits clarity. Just as he is clear to himself, so he will be clear to anyone who desires it; he will allow anyone to see to the depths [*bis in den Grund*] with the same clarity. Whoever conceals himself wants either to defraud [*betrügen*] or to deceive; the moral [person] does not want that—and he is no pious fraud. The moral [person] wants nothing of another person if it cannot take place through *clear insight*; that is his own intention. Or perhaps someone might know that the sight of what is within him would anger or tempt others; but that is not the situation for the moral [person], the sight of whom can only edify (IV/6, 139).

3. HALLE: To the extent that it is a concern of the state [*dem Staat daran liegt*], other means are provided to it for bringing people to truthfulness: honor, fear, etc. (IV/6, 139).

The first claim is clear: knowing falsehood is *absolute, unconditional immorality*, since it denies to others that toward which we ought to strive, as the only means for morality in them, i.e., correct knowledge. There could be no case in which *this* [denial] could be the goal of morality, since it posits others simply as instruments and as incapable of knowledge.[4] No one who considers the matter properly could ever lie without clearly exposing before his own eyes his immorality; hence the psychological phenomenon [*Erscheinung*] of the feeling of shame [*Entehrung*], vilification, and cowardice that lies bring with them.[5]

It is, therefore, quite natural that the most bitter conflict has broken out between the two dispositions (i.e., the moral and the immoral) regarding the main point. From time immemorial the immoral disposition has applied cleverness and sophistry in order to finagle [*erschleichen*] an exception to this and other prohibitions, or at least to introduce [the idea of] a white lie [*Nothlüge*], as if for it this prohibition were the most offensive thing possible [*allerärgerlichste*], however continually and forcefully they may be countered by the other party.

Whoever is well intentioned toward universal morality has held firm regarding this prohibition, *which is valid unconditionally and without exception*. Nothing promotes the development of morality in a human being as surely as the habit of strict truthfulness, and were it only that this were a universal maxim of education [*Erziehung*], things would be quite different for the human species. Speaking the truth, whatever the danger, immediately develops in a person the feeling and awareness of his higher self, | sublimely [elevated] above all earthly consequences, one that is incapable of

---

4. [Original:] Es kann gar keinen Fall geben, wo *dies* Zwek seyn könne, denn es sezt den andern geradezu also Werkzeug, der Sittlichkeit, u. der Erkenntniß unfähig.

5. HALLE: Commonly it is said that there is not only one virtue but rather four cardinal virtues, among which truthfulness is also counted. Knowing falsehood is absolute, formal immorality. There could be no case in which it could be a goal to incite others to falsehood. Any knowing lie within the mind [*Gemüthe*] is already the appearance of immediate immorality. This is already psychologically apparent by way of the feeling of shame (IV/6, 139–140).

foundering or of mingling with sensuousness; everything good and moral is joined to this higher self.

(4) *Simplicity* [*Einfachheit*], which follows on its own accord from this inner truthfulness and is, to a certain extent, one with it. *Others* seek for themselves many skills [*viele Künste*], imagining now this one and now that one as present goals and needs may demand, altogether lacking any conceivable connection or comprehensive unity to sustain them: a dissolute, disordered, and incomprehensible manifold assembled out of pieces. Not so the moral [person]. He remains ever identical with himself throughout the whole course of his life, which thus is completely clear and comprehensible | to anyone who possesses the key to it within himself. He always follows the voice of conscience in intending the goal, possesses a single life [*hat ein Leben*], and acts only for it. {He does} whatever is commanded simply and without ruminating [*ohne Klügeln*], remaining inert [*leblos*] whenever something is not commanded or there is no command. This principle takes possession of him and flows out into him [*fließt ab in ihm*]. It is, therefore, quite far from his manner of thinking and an expression of immorality to seek to extend [*auszeihen*] duties, as if on an adventure. {Those who do so} have no knowledge of duty or of where they belong. Duties are not *freely* thought up [*ausgedacht*] nor borrowed [*übernommen*]; instead, the task is to dedicate oneself to the inner compelling voice. (One has said mockingly that {one can} think about having a character out of boredom. Entirely correct: the character becomes who we are). Concerning *means*, the one, fixed law, [namely,] to act only from knowledge and conviction, and in no other way, is what guides him. What is not possible through this means is morally impossible and ought not to happen.

This is the place to completely eradicate, at least from your understanding, an error on which I have already remarked wherever possible. {The moral person only avails himself} of moral means; he avails himself [*bedient er sich*] of *knowledge*, willing only in this way; | [he does not avail himself of] *compulsion* or *deception*. One other thing remains in the store of human folly, [namely,] *miracle*. A miracle in this sense (and it may be that there is no other sense) is the bringing about of morality through a *physical* means.

{Whoever clings to the idea of a miracle thinks that} morality ought to be brought about [*soll sich machen*] as a *natural occurrence,* through the obscure causality of the fundamental concept [*Grundbegriffs*], not through knowledge and freedom in the sphere of clear {consciousness}. Nature in its entirety is the expression of the very same concept, the moral development of the human species within it is possible, or as possible as it ought to be; as it is placed within nature, freedom ought to intervene there and take up its task. A great miracle has thereby occurred and occurs for all time; the sensible world is this miracle. Who wants a new miracle? What does such a person want? If I may be permitted to use the expression, he wants to make morality more possible than it is [*noch mögliches machen, als sie es ist*]; he wants to restrict the sphere of freedom to expand the unfreedom that existed previously at the expense of freedom and to *turn* human beings through a natural mechanism into what they are *supposed to make themselves through freedom,* in consequence of the concept in its twofold legislation! For this freedom, which rebels against its whole sphere and wants to grant this sphere a higher law, of which there is none, through some obscurity, is defiance against the moral law. The moral [person] obeys the law just as it is and wills that all of humanity obey it. He therefore does not believe in any particular miracle, for such an assumption shrinks [*ist verkleinend*] before the majesty of the law and contradicts belief in it. He does not want this for himself or for others, for any such will | is disobedient. He would therefore be the last person to do that. |

Briefly put, the world, just as it is, is the sphere of our duty. To want to have it otherwise is to want to have it otherwise regarding one's duty. This, however, cannot coexist with a will that is absorbed by duty [*in der Pflicht aufgegangen ist*].

{I have} promised {to present} how the moral [person] reveals himself in his *external* actions. His will is the will of the concept, whose will here below is the *morality of all* and the *means* thereto; it is obvious how one's fellow human beings are, without exception, embraced by this disposition. I would, therefore, have to further *define* external actions in the sphere of common human occupations [*Berufs*] and to show how [the moral person] would appear there; [I would have to] provide as it were a particular *doctrine of duties*, which of course would only be a particular sphere of the appearance of morality within a particular sphere of life.

Lecture 27

(August 10, 1812)

I provided this premise after the discovery of the system, though at that time I did not have the concept of such a chapter clearly in mind. While reflecting on my own during the preparation of this [chapter], I found that I would be unable to say anything new in it that has not already been said quite often and that follows on its own from the established principles for anyone who is able to simply make the inferences. But I find it very difficult, indeed, well-nigh impossible, to present something about which I am not assured of fresh powers of thought and discovery; the same holds when I cannot place my hope in posing such a task to [the students]. I therefore excuse myself from [presenting] this chapter, all the more so since I can communicate it to them in print: p. 439, §26 [of the *System of Ethics*].[1] (If you have listened to me attentively, you can leave the rest unread.) |

In lieu of this, I want to provide an appendix [*Anhang*] in which I hope to furnish a perspective that is very important and that, in fact, fits quite well with one of the needs of the age.

Everyone should work toward the morality of every person who comes into his sphere of efficacy [*Wirkungssphäre*], both through deed, which is to be held out to another as an example for his *consideration* [*Begreifen*], and also through

---

1. See GA 1/5, 285–287. The passage referred to here introduces the final section of the work, in which Fichte discusses particular duties as expressions of the universal duty to promote the goal of reason as such.

word; above all, though, [he should work] toward his own *conviction* and *insight*. There is a reciprocity [*Wechselwirkung*] via concepts. But all reciprocity via concepts must proceed from a common principle. Where such a [principle] is not present, there is endless conflict and understanding is quite impossible. This common principle *is* given to the moral vocation of all.[2]

This should always be brought to awareness from the root up [*von der Wurzel aus*] (as must be the case with educating someone for being a rational person [*Erziehung zum vernünftiger Mensch*]), though it may be a particular occupation [*Geschäft*] and may not be possible in the appropriate way [*füglich*] in the midst of other occupations; or perhaps [it may be possible] only occasionally. It is therefore to be wished that one could already count on *consciousness* in each case, and that certain general formulas and modes of speech were in use, whereby one could in each case correct [others]; i.e., [that there were] certain basic moral concepts about which one could assume that all were in agreement. [This would be] a common, fundamental moral consciousness of the entire species in which it is already a complete unity, just as by nature there is a collective [consciousness] of the sensible world. Just as in the latter case one can say "look there" and can expect something with certainty, so one could, in the former case, say "think about that," etc.

This would be something to wish for.

Since there is no other vocation during the collective life span of our species than *unification* [*Vereinigung*], it is to be expected that, as long as [the species] has stood for a while in a coherent, continuous reciprocity, its life has not been futile, and such a point of unification | in *insight* and in *action* will be achieved. {I said} in *continual reciprocity*, such that there would be, as it were, an eternal, living memory of the species that links everything new with what is old and thereby determines it. {This is} the historical human species, [and] it is conditional upon peaceful

---

2. CAUER: Now such a common principle within all human beings is the moral vocation *of all*, to the extent that all individuality is annulled [*aufgehoben*] and all are only one organic life.

coexistence, transmission [*Ueberlieferung*] and the means for it, as in the case of a scripture. What is best in such a history [*Historie*] is not what one *learns* but rather the extent to which one is born into it through one's ancestors. Cultivated humanity [*kultivirte Menschheit*] belongs to history, and acquiring a history or acquiring a culture [*Kultur*] (where no step that has been achieved is lost) are really one and the same thing. Agreement about action is set down in custom [*Sitte*] (not to steal, to kill, etc., which is what the natural human being [*Naturmensch*] who is not, as a rule, historical, does), expressed through the law, which till now has been hardly anything but the expression of custom and has been formed gradually rather than being willed on the basis of *a priori* concepts. The community that is comprehended by this is the *state*. We will not deal with this here.

Agreement in *insight* is called the *creed* [*Symbol*],[3] and, on this assumption, the community (of those who believe in the creed) that is comprehended by it is called the community of believers: *the church*.

This is the universal *precondition* [*Vorbegriff*]. The pertinent question that I want to answer is this: to what extent does the creed bind the moral will in moral reciprocity | with others? At issue is not a [theory of] duty but a theory of the appearance of the moral will, i.e., of the will of the concept, which is assumed to be absolutely [*schlechthin*] unerring. How does this relate to the creed? |

II/13, 382

StA 384

---

3. German has various terms that are roughly equivalent to the English word "creed," for example, *Glaubensbekenntnis*, *Konfession*, or *Kredo*. Fichte here (as elsewhere, e.g., in the 1798 *System der Sittenlehre*) uses the more unusual and archaic *Symbol*, which is ultimately of Greek derivation. Fichte's choice likely reflects, at least in part, his view that historical creeds are "enveloping images [*einkleidenden Bilder*]" that help to render the concept of the supersensible intelligible to sensuous beings (see GA 1/5, 219). Fichte may also have in mind Kant's discussion in §59 of the *Critique of the Power of Judgment*, "On Beauty as a Symbol of Morality" (AA 5: 351–354), where Kant carefully distinguishes different ways of linking sensible intuitions with nonsensible concepts. Fichte's general interest in the nature of religious symbolism is evidenced by his discussion of the ancient Greek Palladium (a religious icon that appears in Homer and that played an important role in Roman state religion) in the *Staatslehre* lectures of 1813 (GA II/16, 37). I have elected to render the term as "creed" in light of the specifically religious connotation that *Symbol* has in the present lectures.

(1) What can the creed contain? [Answer:] that which is given in some shape through the moral consciousness, as though via an eye.

This much has been made very clear by way of our entire investigation, [namely,] that what is important for morality is not some qualitative and material deed [*Thun*] but rather a certain disposition [*Gesinnung*].[4] [It has likewise become clear] that this attitude [*Sinnesweise*], this, as it were, newly implanted eye, brings with it its own system of cognition [*Erkenntnißsystem*], its own world, just as the natural consciousness brings with it its own [world], the sensible world. The former is something supersensible, the vocation of the human being [*die Bestimmung des Menschen*], the relationship of this earthly creature to something higher.[5] It is nothing but this, and this is precisely the content of the moral consciousness. Philosophy also contains it, and [indeed] ought to do so.

(2) How is the creed established [*Wie kommt das Symbol zu Stande*]? Let this be answered in the most general way. The concept breaks through into consciousness somewhere in the world. Just as surely as it is the concept, [it does so] within a moral consciousness, along with the mandate [*Auftrage*] that it be communicated and disseminated as widely as possible.[6, 7] Just as surely as this is an *original*

---

4. CAUER: It has emerged from the entire course of our investigation that what is important is not a material deed but rather an inner conviction [*Ueberzeugung*].

5. Fichte's reference here to the "vocation of the human being" recalls, most immediately, Fichte's 1800 work of that title (see GA I/6, 145–312), which culminates in a section dealing with "faith [*Glaube*]" as the completion or perfection of the moral disposition.

6. CAUER: Somewhere, the higher concept breaks through into consciousness *through itself* (no individual can elevate himself to morality on his own). But just as surely as that which has broken through is the *moral concept*, it carries with it the command that it should be communicated.

7. HALLE: How is the creed established? To answer in the most general way: the higher concept breaks through to consciousness somewhere in the world on its own power. No one can elevate himself to it. Human beings are born in sensible intuition. Moral [intuition] is an event; but, just as surely as it is the moral concept that has broken through, it carries with it the command that it be communicated (IV/6, 142).

breakthrough, this occurs by means of something that is, as yet, nowhere present in the world, in an incomprehensible way, not connected to any previously existing member, i.e., [it happens] via genius [*genialisch*], {as} revelation.[8] We can leave undecided just how clearly and completely this system of morality will be revealed at the beginning. Since the human species develops gradually, it is not to be expected that it will occur straightaway in the highest clarity and completeness. As this [person] acts, he will *communicate* and be understood by others as well as he can be. The grounds of conviction with which it is set out [*dem es sich anlegt*] can be nothing other than one's own *moral sense* [*sittliche Sinn*] of it. Conviction and understanding can reach no further at any time than does this moral sense for those to whom it is communicated. The goal of communication is that an agreement [*Einverständniß*] among many people regarding morality be established; if it is established, then what is essential has been achieved. The first person who communicates may, of course, raise everyone to the clarity and breadth of knowledge that he himself possesses, but, if this is not possible, it is always better that they grant him one thing to which what is higher can afterward be linked; he must be satisfied with that.[9] The creed is in no way the doctrine [*Lehre*] of the person through whom the revelation of the concept first comes to pass, either concerning what he has within him or what he is able to express in language, even granting the assumption that [such language] has never yet been used for this type of communication. Instead, [the creed] is what even the least of those who are in agreement actually hears and understands [*einsieht*], which is something one can assume of anyone whom we meet that is a member of the church. What a gulf [*Kluft*] exists between the genuine doctrine of revelation and the

---

8. HALLE: One cannot speak of a product of genius [*vom Genialischen*] in philosophy or in any science, because what is there already exists and is not created out of nothing (IV/6, 142).

9. [Fichte's marginal note:] E.g., there is something that is extramundane [*überweltliches*], be it merely a natural force [*Naturgewalt*]; this is already a point of contact [*Anknüpfungspunkt*].

creed of the church that has been erected upon it! (If you want an example: the doctrine of Jesus in John's Gospel, for the unbiased, for those who have not already been taken in by a creed, versus [the doctrines of] dogmatic Christian theologians.)[10]

Furthermore, it is clear that the doctrine can be better understood and grasped with higher clarity and perfection by [different] individuals in a great variety of levels. Do the insights of these individuals constitute the creed? Obviously not, since [the creed consists] only in what is agreed upon by all. Just as surely as it is a creed, some truth belongs to it, e.g., that there *is a God*. Both the doctrine and the improved knowledge agree on this. | This claim is, however, further determined by ignorance and a lack of understanding, not really through the creed but rather through creedal human beings [*die symoblischen Menschen*]. The creed only allows for this because it can do nothing to block it. Both the doctrine and the improved knowledge do not take on this further determination; they clearly recognize its groundlessness, and they replace it with something better. There is a great gulf between it and the creed. What should one do?

---

10. Fichte's choice of this example reflects his own view that the Gospel of John (and other parts of the Johannine corpus in the New Testament) contains the authentic core of Christian teaching. Fichte elaborates on this point at some length in his 1806 *Anweisung zum seeligen Leben* (GA I/9, 1–212). See also Fichte's discussion in Lecture 12.

Lecture 28

(August 12, 1812)

Every creed contains knowledge from the standpoint of morality; it is always based on a revelation to one or more inspired individuals. [The creed] contains that about which all who believe in this revelation and are instructed by it (i.e., the church) are in agreement (they have been instructed and by means of it have progressed; that is sufficient).

Some, however, have said that such a creed stands far below the genuine doctrine that is intended by the revelation, as well as below the faith (in a moral respect) of the cultured members of the church, within the sphere of the doctrine of revelation or perhaps even beyond this. This [supposedly] deeper standpoint might consist not only in imperfection and a lack of clear knowledge but rather in an | actual error stemming from the former. If, for example, the correct cognition that there is a God were further determined as follows: there is an arbitrary ruler of the world [*Weltherrscher*] who issues laws without any conceivable reason, which we must uphold because he is mightier, and things go badly for us if we are disobedient—then this is an error, and, like all errors, it is contrary to morality. How could I now say that those who are more cultured agree with the creed [in this case]? Answer: they agree only with what is true in the creed (in this case, [with the claim that] there is a God, something supersensible as such [*ein übersinnliches überhaupt*]), not with the further, immoral, determination [of the creed]. |

The extent to which the creed binds the moral person in reciprocity with members of his church becomes clear on this basis. It is not that he ought to be compelled to believe what he knows to be erroneous, nor to take pains to believe it or to provide it with some meaning, nor that his conscience should be troubled by it! Even in the darkest age the most zealous champions of the rights of the church did not go this far; they left the conscience at liberty. Nor [would he be bound by the creed] *to teach* what he knows to be false. He does not want [what he knows to be false] to be taught, nor would he even allow it to be if he could do something to hinder it! Since he knows that this is absolutely immoral, how could this [desire] coexist with his living zeal for the moral formation [*Bildung*] of all? He would not venture to contest [*bestreite*] it at the risk of weakening and overturning the truth that is mixed in with the error. This danger is, as a rule, always present. If, through his contesting of the erroneous definition of God, belief in God were eroded in the minds of those whose God depends upon this erroneous definition and can only be conceived of by means of it, then something that has already been achieved by the community of believers would be negated. [In that case] a member who was only loosely or lightly associated with the community would be expelled from it. Someone who is concerned solely with morality, not with theoretical clarity and consistency, would never be answerable to his conscience. (Later we will consider more deeply cases in which it is permissible, indeed obligatory, to exit [*auszugehen*] [the community] on account of theoretical clarity, since it is a means for moral illumination.) The moral [person] takes everyone as he is; but those errors belong to someone's unavoidable nature [*Seyn*], from which [the moral person] seeks to raise him up. He would, however, never dare to abandon a connection with moral | knowledge. Instruction [*Unterricht*] in the spirit of morality within the church would obviously never teach what is plainly erroneous to the teacher himself. Nor would the teacher contest it; rather he links his instruction to that which is true within this mixture | with falsity, and he elevates it. If such instruction is useful, it is useful for most and ultimately for all.

In this way, falsehood is expunged from the general faith without being noticed, since it can no longer coexist with the elevated and expanded cognition of truth, and not a single member of the church will believe it any longer. The creed has been changed and elevated, and it is constantly elevated through the perpetuation of such instruction and of the doctrine of revelation that lies at its basis. Thus it approximates ever more closely the faith of the cultured. The creed is perfectible, and it is the principal goal of the church that it be continually perfected [*vervollkommnt*].

This goal of the church is only attainable on the condition that those appointed to teach are not held captive by [*gefangen*] the creed (for then it would be corrupted and the church would fall into decline [*verfallen*], as many historical examples make evident). Instead [they must be] above it. Above every creed and above the church itself lies science; the established perfectibility of the creed, as well as of the church, are conditioned by the existence of a scientific public in the fold [*Schooße*] of the church. Ecclesiastical teachers must be formed [*gebildet*] by science and must themselves be members of this scientific public.

Who in our context has opposed such obvious principles, and do they still oppose them? At what point does the opposing party | deny the principle and set up a different one? The opposing party would consist of those who assert the absolute inalterability of the creed. There are such people. We have said that the truth of the doctrine of faith that is set forth be attested to inwardly by each person in his own moral sense. We know of no other means of verification or for connecting [*Anknüpfung*] [people to it]. {We possess only} inner proof. They, on the other hand, want to base faith on the authority of testimony and make the proof external—asking, as in a legal investigation, about the number and integrity of the witnesses and about their capacity for knowledge. In this case, where there is no inner criterion of truth nor any organ of knowledge that arises of its own accord, the [original] statement has to remain unaltered in just the way it was [initially] made, because it is proven true only with this content. From this perspective, the external history of the founding revelation acquires a value in the face of which its content almost entirely vanishes, because faith is grounded on this history. On our view, on the other hand, it is not important in itself who may have first said what. | The statement is true for us now, even if no one in the world had ever said it; we rest content with our own conviction. Inner acceptance of something as being true does not arise on the basis of {external} proof; only, perhaps, an absence of disagreement or a repetition of the words does so. The only thing that is proven [this way] is that so and so said it and perhaps accepted it as being true; but what concern of ours is this other person? Either an inner conviction develops by accident in carrying out such a proof (as we say, and as has been reported previously), or it does not, in which case we have in fact gained nothing but historical knowledge, which | is of no use to us. One has been satisfied in this ecclesiastical system with such external confessions all the more so because they have been used to strengthen the historical proof and thus to increase the number of people who will make this confession in the future. The [opponents'] claim would be that that which *all* have believed to be true at *all* times is true, and you individuals who would dare to contest it regard yourselves as cleverer than all of them. An imposing authority was rightly brought to bear, and the poorest knowledge was established as a yardstick [*Maasstab*] for the confession and as an eternally enduring creed. Indeed, if it can be discovered (more on this later) what it is that all have believed at all times and ought to believe henceforth in all eternity on account of their basic determination, this may be true. But, just as certainly as the supersensible only develops gradually into actuality, so the latest revelation of God is always the correct one, which ought to be brought to all people, in comparison with which what even the most cultured have believed is worth little. In addition to this, [those who hold this view] would have to arbitrarily date this whole of time from some point. The author of the fourth book of Cicero's *de natura Deorum* humorously satirized this. The *pontifex maximus*, Cotta, proves | that there are gods *in plurali* because this has been believed by all at all times in an uninterrupted series. The Jews, apparently, would be an exception, which

| | does not mean much in itself, but which, if one sees cor-
StA 392 | rectly, renders [Cotta's claim] false.¹ |

II/13, 387 | One should not respond to objections based on such belief in authority, for we simply do not accept | this proof. A church based on such belief in authority can, occa-
StA 393–395 | sionally and by accident, develop | moral knowledge in human beings, just as everything in the given world can and should, otherwise it is not tolerated by God—but its
II/13, 388 | means do not at all fit this end. | [Such a church is merely the
StA 396 | propagator | of a historical tradition that is not important in itself. Therefore it is not really a church. Only that which has a direct effect on inner conviction [belongs to] a church. Those who, within this historical tradition, have no choice but to retain this history of revelation along with its content have at least the possibility of preserving a true church that is joined to it and are to that extent links in the chain of the progressive formation [*Fortbildung*] of the human species. I will touch more deeply later on the last and utmost
StA 397 | thing that hides behind this belief in authority.² |

---

1. Fichte is referring to *M. Tulli Ciceronis de natura deorum liber quartus. E pervetusto codice Ms. Membranaceo nunc primum edit P. Seraphinus, Ord. Fr. Min. Bononiae*. This work, which appeared in 1811, purported to be a lost fourth book of Cicero's *De natura deorum*. In actuality, the author was Hermann Heimart Cludius (1754–1835), a Göttingen-educated theologian and pastor.

2. CAUER: In order for a church to be assured that it contains a real progress of moral cognition, it must include a scientific circle, part of which deals with what is historical and part with what is philosophical.

Lecture 29

(August 13, 1812)

We found that a scientific public must exist within the fold of the church. It must be arranged [*bearbeiten*] into two branches, the historical and the philosophical.

First of all, with respect to the historical [branch] of the church, it has just now been shown that nothing immediately depends on the history of *revelation* and its propagation via the church with regard to communicating it to the uneducated members of the church, insofar as this is an ancillary issue that, as such, must be handled differently than the main goal of inner conviction. However, in certain cases, [the revelation] could be *capable of being communicated* indirectly, and a lot might depend on [the historical] branch with respect to the education [*Bildung*] of the teacher. This could, for example, happen in cases where literary documents [*Urkunden*] concerning the revelation upon which the church is founded exist and, since in that case there could be no other appropriate way, these are set forth as the genuine creed for which the current interpretation of the actual creed merely strives. These [documents] stand as the genuine [*eigentlich*], perfect creed, and all other creeds acquire their validity from agreement with them, as is the case, for example, in the familiar Protestant church, something that few Protestant theologians would have the effrontery to deny. If an equally authentic interpretation that partakes of all the rights of immediate revelation stands alongside of it, then nothing more can be done to begin with than to overturn this interpretation, as our Reformers quite rightly did in a way that fully agrees with the laws of the progress of culture [*Bildung*]. Now if, as some think, they only had something against the present interpretation and not the principle, and had wanted to posit theirs as equally eternal | and the documents as an equally valid creed in its place, then this would be inconsistent to the highest degree, and we would have to proceed against their interpretation just as they had done according to their own principle.[1] | If it were the case (i.e., if there were somehow further reasons to believe, as I, for example, have freely admitted there are) that no document has ever been completely and rightly understood since it came into being, and that therefore its true content has never been set down in any possibly extant interpretation, then everything must depend on a future teacher understanding it correctly in order to increase his own knowledge and to raise the creed that he has inherited to this [level of] understanding and thence also others' creeds. This may not be possible without the study of languages and of history. If, for example, one ascribed to the founder of our Christian religion that he was inspired by God, and by means of this inspiration was wrenched from every link with worlds that came before or after in the natural progression of education [*Bildung*], [i.e.,] was an exceptional moral genius like those of a different kind who we also recognize among different peoples [*Völkern*] of antiquity—which would be the least that anyone who conversed with him would verbally confess—then one should not assume it to be simply [*schlechthin*] impossible that he could have had insight into many things that we, despite our culture and our philosophy, still do not know at this very hour and that we could learn from him. In that case it would be quite possible that one could adopt the goal of impartially studying every document simply in order to understand and to learn from it. Here, too, what is important is not *who* {said something} but rather *what* {was said}; whatever we come to understand should only be valid for us to the extent that we understand it and convince

---

1. CAUER: However, were the INTERPRETATION of these documents contrary to their content, then it would be cast away.

ourselves of its truth, regardless of the fact that we could not have discovered it on our own. |

Given that someone did not share this opinion, or saw some other way to increase his own knowledge, this text is always, *ex hypothesi*, the established [*stehende*] creed in which the church believes, and it will always be necessary to be familiar with its content in order to recognize once more in it what has been discovered in some other way and to resolutely demonstrate what is in it for the members of the church.

The second part of the arrangement of the scientific [public within the church] is *philosophical*.

Philosophy, just in case it is complete in itself [*in sich zu Ende ist*], encompassing the system of knowing, i.e., a *Wissenschaftslehre*, contains among other things the same content possessed by every creed and every possible revelation, i.e., cognition from a moral point of view. The formal grounds of its cognition, however, are entirely different. [In the former case, the formal ground] is the *moral sense*, the feeling of agreement with the inspired individual insofar as [the revelation] is communicated—genius [*Genialität*], a hiatus. [In the latter case, i.e., in philosophy, the formal ground is] the universal interior eye, i.e., *seeing*, whereas there it is *feeling*. It is well known that the interior eye | concerns the *genesis* of everything that is factual. {Philosophy} simply [*schlechthin*] allows what is factual to arise, which goes also for morality itself and everything contained in it. [Philosophy] is clear; [it consists] entirely in *that which is clear*, encompassing the organic faith [*umfassend das organische Glaube*]. [Philosophy provides] the content of every possible revelation in its organic completeness and clarity, and therefore it is the perfection and goal of the progress of the church. | ({I want to exhibit} the opposition {between philosophical knowledge} and revelation as [that between] sight and feeling.)

(1) Sight [*Sehe*] and feeling are absolute opposites. Philosophy must therefore venture to tear human beings free from every sphere {of feeling}, regardless of the risk; nothing else matters to it. [Philosophy] is purely theoretical. It must grant the creed a hypothetical status [*Das Symbol muß er hypothetisch verlassen*]. How could a person dare

to offer up a different philosophy with respect to morality? This does not really happen.[2] The moral concept struggles for clarity [*ringt nach Klarheit*] and thus for philosophy. That which breaks into the individual during this struggle is not external freedom but rather *the concept itself*. Such a person looks around for external instruction or tuition. The drive for philosophy must arise in each person himself and is assumed in all instruction. Nothing else matters, and the person remains just as much a believing member of the church [*kirchengläubig*], or just as sensuous and unbelieving, as he was before. In the latter case his unbelief would only acquire *words*. This momentarily sad, vexing situation, which no individual may accept, counts as nothing within
StA 401 the great household | of divine providence, and *those* who have brought it about through this drive [for philosophy] are responsible for it. A clear [thinking] person who is sensuous and unbelieving is always worth more to the whole than a dull-witted, mute person is by himself. Unbelief always develops toward its own annihilation.[3]

(2) Moral faith, where it attains to true philosophy, develops itself to the point of clarity and of the drive to want to see. Philosophy assumes it; there must already be an object that it wants to see in a clear light. But moral faith comes into factual existence only through revelation and inspiration [*Inspiration*]. Therefore, all philosophy, despite the fact that it is, according to its form, elevated above every church, nevertheless, as far as its factual being goes, proceeds from the church and from its revealed principle. The philosopher therefore is and remains a member of the church, for he is necessarily brought forth from its fold and takes from it his point of departure.

(3) It has been asked whether reason (rationality or philosophy) is the judge in matters of faith, the touchstone

2. [Original:] Wie kann es nun ein Mensch, bei Sittlichkeit, wagen, einem andern Ph[ilosophie] anzurtragen? Dies geschieht auch eigentlich nicht.

3. CAUER: If the person is a believer, then he remains a believer; if he is sensuous and unbelieving, then he remains this way—if, in the latter condition, he takes something from philosophy, it is only that his unbelief acquires words and language. The sad situation [*Schade*] that could thus come to be is charged to the account of divine world governance.

Lecture 29

for the correctness of every putative revelation, and, despite the fact that now every educated person may agree about what the answer should be, there often seems to be a lack of courage for expressing this view outright. | I, however, think that it is important to express it clearly, and, moreover, that I must express it to you who, just in case you are convinced, should disseminate it further. The premises have already been established. If philosophy contains, in an organic unity and with perfect clarity, all of moral cognition, as the content of all possible revelations, of all creeds, and of all ecclesiastical faith, then there can be no doubt that it, and it alone, | is the highest judge, and that everything that contradicts it is wrong and must be annulled and left behind through continual progress. To that extent, the doctrine of philosophy regarding the supersensible is the pure faith toward which every ecclesiastical doctrine and creed must be elevated during the course of time.

Those who contradict this claim understand both it and, in particular, the words "philosophy" and "reason," in a different sense. For them reason and philosophy are merely the faculty of ratiocination [*RäsonirVermögen*] about the sensible world, since a different type of ratiocination has not yet occurred to them, and they judge based on their experience. We grant and say along with them, among other places in these lectures, whatever bad thing they might say about the blindness of this merely sensuous understanding regarding the supersensible; let them judge as they want. They assume that [the supersensible] is a completely different world, without any connection or unifying bridge [with this one], and that one cannot arrive at it with any combination, progressive improvement, or clarification of the sensible. [Moreover, they assume that] one must be elevated to it through a miracle, through a leap over [the sensible]. We grant all this and preach it just like they do.

We also grant that one cannot arrive at true philosophy without this uplifting [*Erhebung*], and that philosophy itself rests upon the factual ground of a revelation. But we do not agree with them that philosophy is nothing but the combination of sensuous concepts and can only ask them to acquire better knowledge of it and henceforth not to meddle with something completely foreign to them. | What would those who contradict our claim, when it is understood well and properly, have to assume? They say, "God has spoken, and so what more is left for a human being to decide?" This is the uttermost height of their proof of authority. They do not consider that someone who was not himself there when this happened could very well doubt their own or their witnesses' credibility, and that, in doing so, he is not chastening God but rather *them*, regarding the lie or the error. Can they not consider for themselves that they are not God nor could they become God? And how do things stand with the assertion that they want to dupe us in God's name, should [the revelation] contain something incomprehensible | to reason, i.e., a mystery? They assume that God could speak to us otherwise than through his eternal Word, his absolute image through which the world was created, that he could appear or not, that he could appear one way or another, and that this divine image does not bring with it its absolute criterion, i.e., reason, the very reason of which philosophy is itself the factual appearance. [This is what] they suppose or rather do not suppose, since such ideas have never yet been dragged into the thick darkness of their superstition.

The world is God's image, and just as [God] *exists*, so does the world in every way [*ganz*], and it cannot come into being; no new being can be created, though the one being always develops itself into consciousness. What do these [people] possess as a god or as a world? A world that is complete and subsists for itself without God, or if one considers what some teach, one that subsists through a devil. A god who once upon a time intervened arbitrarily in the world (such are their miracles) and brought forth something in it that never really recurs, in that it does not | belong to its concept but rather must be retained as the remembrance of an empty fact (such are their mysteries).

It is to be expected that, given the state of their case, they would protest against the judgeship of reason.

The application of philosophy to the improvement of the creed can be carried out easily and has been already in passing.

I said [that this] accords with the age, for superstition will not die yet but rather seems to have come into existence again through a type of reaction; particularly among

Protestants, one hears many extreme things said about the church and its power.

I have also expressed myself on this point, which may often be a shock to the conscience. As far as I know, there is nothing else of significance that remains [to be said], and so I conclude these lectures.

German–English Glossary

Abbild	likeness
Abdruck	imprint, impression, copy, replica
Abfluß	effluence
ableiten (*Ableitung*)	to derive, deduce
Absatz	precipitate
absetzen (*Absetzung*)	to deposit, precipitate
Absicht	intention, purpose, aim, target
Allgemeingültig	universally valid, obtaining universally
Ansicht	view, point of view, perspective
Ausdruck	expression
Begreifen	to conceive, conceive of, comprehend
Begriff	concept, idea
bestimmen	to determine, define
Bestimmung	determination, definition, qualification, vocation, defining vocation
Beweiß	proof, demonstration
bilden	to image, form, cultivate, educate
Bild	image
bildlich	representational
Bildlichkeit	representationality

Bildung	formation, cultivation, education, culture
Empirie	experience, empirical domain
Facticität	factuality, factual reality
faktisch	factual
Faktum, Tatsache	fact
gebildet	educated, cultured
Gedanke	thought, idea
Geist	spirit, intelligence, mind
geistig	intellectual, spiritual
Geistigkeit	intelligence, intelligibility
Gesicht	idea, something that is seen
Grundsatz	principle
Grundseyn	being a ground
kräftig	powerful, forceful, dynamic
lebendig	vital, living
Legendigkeit	vitality, life
Mensch	human being, person
Menschheit	humanity
mittelbar	indirect, indirectly
Mittelbarkeit	indirectness
Moral, Sittlichkeit, Moralität	morality
Nachbild	afterimage, copy
Princip	principle
Principiat	that which is produced or brought about by a principle

Reflex	reflection, reflective awareness
Reflexionspunkt	angle of vision, perspective, point of view
Sehe	sight
Schein	illusion
Sittenlehre	theory of ethics
Voraussetzung (voraussetzen)	presupposition, assumption
Vorbild	paradigm
vollziehen	to actualize, activate, enact
Wechselwirkung	reciprocity, reciprocal action
Werkzeug	instrument, tool
willen (Wille, Willen)	to will (will, act of will)
Wollen	willing, act of will
Wissenslehre	theory of knowing
Zweck	end, goal, purpose

Index

a priori concepts, 60, 125, 155
absolute, the, 18, 44, 74
absolute being, 4, 17, 39, 48n1, 51n8
absolute concept, xix, 5, 74, 96n4
  appearance and, 54–55, 66–67, 74, 77, 80, 81, 120
  duty and, 59, 60, 127. *See also* absolute duty
  ethics and, 142
  external criterion for, 56–57
  freedom and, xx, 23
  and the I, xx, 23, 54–56, 59–61, 66–67, 85
  reason and, 55
absolute consciousness, 3–4
absolute content of the pure concept, 18
absolute creativity, 12–13, 27, 39, 41, 56
absolute determination of the I, xx. *See also* absolute self-determination
absolute duty, 59, 83, 116. *See also* absolute concept: duty and
absolute eye, 96
absolute form of morality, 125
absolute freedom, 17, 41
absolute ground, 4, 50
absolute image, 6, 55, 74n7, 122
absolute principle, 79, 94, 110
absolute self-determination, xx, 12, 16–17, 22, 29, 31, 35, 39
absolute unity, 29, 38, 116n7

absolute will, 83, 84n1, 85–87, 91, 92n3, 125, 133, 142, 145
  duty and, 80
"Accidental Thoughts on a Sleepless Night" (Fichte), x–xii
acts of will. *See* will; willing
actuality, 17, 132
  of appearance, 67, 73
  of being a ground, 12, 13
  and the I, 67, 72n1, 73, 78, 104, 132
  willing and, 29
actualization
  freedom and, 42n9
  ground and, 21, 35, 41
  and the I, 28, 29, 37
Addresses to the German Nation (Fichte), vii, viii, x, xi, xxii
affection (*Neigung*), 140, 142
appearance, 71–75, 85, 100–101, 110
  absolute concept and, 54–55, 66–67, 74, 77, 80, 81, 120
  of the absolute image, 122
  actuality of, 67, 73
  of appearance, 74, 103n1
  and the concept, 71–75
  of the concept, xxi, 66, 72, 73n5, 74–75, 77, 95n3, 96, 127
  form of, 51, 72, 100nn3–4, 101
  freedom and, 54, 66, 110
  of God, 18, 100n4, 110, 113n1, 119–20
  of the I, 78, 83, 84n2, 85, 89, 91, 122n6

appearance *(continued)*
  mere, 56n7, 74, 108
  of the mind, 130
  moral vs. immoral, xx–xxi
  objective, 44, 99, 123n8
  ought and, 57
  real, 100
  of the real, 108nn1–2
  theory of, xx, 54–55, 60, 61, 67
Attempt at a New Presentation of the Wissenschaftslehre, An (Fichte), xviii
authority, xxiii, 161–63

being, 7. *See also* ground
  absolute, 4, 17, 39, 48n1, 51n8
  formal, 43, 97
  objective, 21, 27–28, 30, 34, 71–72, 126
  principle of (*principium essendi*), 101
  theory of, xx, 51, 65
  true, 51, 53, 61, 69, 83
  visibility of, 51
Beyme, K. F., x, xi
Bildlichkeit (representationality), 93, 96, 99, 100n3, 101n5
  as the defining form of appearance, 101

categorical imperative, xx, 5n6, 37, 38, 45
causality, 16, 49n4, 92, 99
  actual, 17, 19
  of the concept, 10n4, 11, 15, 17, 18, 22, 24, 30, 33, 34n4, 35, 37, 39n5, 42n9, 65n1, 66n2, 73, 150
  consciousness and, 10n4, 11, 17, 18, 24, 35, 37, 39n5, 49n4
  ethics and, xxi, 39n5
  freedom and, 16–17, 19, 30, 33, 49n4
  ground and, 11, 37
  and the I, 24, 34n4, 73

  intuition and, 11, 16
  willing and, 30n5
Christianity. *See also* church; creed; John, Gospel of
  God and, 55n3, 65n1, 66n2, 114
  sensible world and, 65n1, 66n2
church, 155, 157–61, 167
  belief in authority and, 163. *See also* authority
  as community of believers, xiii, 155, 160
  ethics and, xxii–xxiii, 62, 160, 163n2
  historical and philosophical branches, 165–70
  Protestant, 165, 171
  revelation, creed, and, xxii–xxiii, 157–59, 161, 163, 165, 167
cognition and ground, 91, 92n3, 167
collective consciousness, 110, 111n8, 120, 154
communication, 109, 157, 165
community, 108–11, 114. *See also* collective consciousness
  of believers, 155, 160
  consciousness and, 107–8, 110, 114
  ethics and, xii–xiii, xiv–xv, xxii, 102n6, 107, 116, 117n8, 141, 155
  freedom and, 96, 102n6, 117n8
  of individuals, 99, 100, 100n2, 101n5, 107, 110
  of I's, xxi, 96–97, 107–8
concept, objective. *See* objective concept
concept, the, 15. *See also* ground: and the concept; pure concept; *specific topics*
  actuality and, 12, 67, 72, 73
  actualization and, 21, 35, 41
  causality of, 10n4, 11, 15, 17, 18, 22, 24, 30, 33, 34n4, 35, 37, 39n5, 42n9, 65n1, 66n2, 73, 150

Index

consciousness and, xx, 3–7, 9, 10, 12, 16, 17, 22, 27–28, 35–40, 57, 79, 83, 94, 113–15, 120, 125n1, 127, 128, 150, 156
  as the ground of itself, 21
  as the ground of the world, xix–xx, 3–7, 8n13, 9–10, 15, 34n3, 44, 66n2
  life of, 19, 24, 28–30, 33, 43, 50, 51, 54–57, 59, 66n2, 67, 71–75, 77–80, 84, 85, 92–94, 99, 115–17, 119, 125, 132, 143n7
  as the only thing that absolutely exists, 47
  power of, 69
  sensible world and, 65n1, 66n2, 84n2
  visibility of, 67, 68, 91
concepts, theory of, xix
conscience, 135
  church and, 160
  voice of, 125n1, 127, 149
consciousness, 3–4, 5nn7–10, 79–80, 96n4, 120–21, 150, 154. *See also* facts of consciousness; self-consciousness
  absolute, 3–4
  causality and, 10n4, 11, 17, 18, 24, 35, 37, 39n5, 49n4
  clear, 62, 128, 129n5
  collective, 110, 111n8, 120, 154
  community and, 107–8, 110, 114
  and the concept, xx, 3–7, 9, 10, 12, 16, 17, 22, 27–28, 35–40, 57, 79, 83, 94, 113–15, 120, 125n1, 127, 128, 150, 156
  duty and, 59–60, 80
  ethics and, 9–10, 11n5, 115, 125n1, 127, 128, 129n5. *See also* moral consciousness
  fivefold structure of, 13
  forms of, 17, 18, 27–28, 39, 107–8, 121
  freedom and, 35–36, 44, 49, 50, 127, 150
  God and, 38, 62, 120, 129n5, 170
  ground and, 3–6, 9–12, 16, 22, 27, 28, 35–36, 39–42
  and the I, xx, 16, 24, 27, 28, 35, 37–40, 46, 54, 55, 79, 80, 83, 93, 94
  intuition and, 11, 27, 28
  life and, xx, 24, 27, 49–50, 55, 93
  moral, xii–xiii, 38–39, 94, 95n3, 122, 154, 156
  objective, 28, 33nn1–2, 35, 39, 44, 50
  ought and, 35, 37, 38, 40–41, 57, 79, 80
  pure concept and, 6–7, 96n4
  willing and, 33nn1–2, 35–36, 40–42, 80, 113–15, 128, 129n5
creativity, absolute, 12–13, 27, 39, 41, 56
creed, xxii, 155–57, 165. *See also* church
  authority and, 161, 162
  ethics and, xii–xiii, xxiii, 159, 160, 167, 169
  faith and, xiii, 159
  God and, 158, 159
  perfectibility, 161
  philosophy and, xiii, xxiii, 167–69
  science and, xii
  terminology, 155n3

Deduced Plan of an Institute of Higher Learning to Be Established in Berlin (Fichte), x–xiii, xvi, xxviii
dialogical process, xi, xiv
duties, doctrines of, 147, 151
duty, xxii, 107, 127, 130
  absolute, 59, 83, 116
  absolute concept and, 59, 60, 127
  command of, 92n3, 132–35, 139
  of the community, 110
  consciousness and, 59–60, 80
  ethics and, 140, 147, 149
  and the I, 83–84

duty *(continued)*
   law of, 116
   theory of, 59–60, 110n6, 155
   will, willing, and, xxi, 59, 60, 80, 91, 116, 121–23, 134, 150

education. *See also* pedagogy; university
   dialogical process, xi, xiv
   education theory and divine education of human species, 52, 62–63
   educational reform, ix–xi
egoism, 108nn1–2
empirical, the, 30, 99, 102n7
empirical I, 31n6, 42n9, 105
eternity, 78–81, 83–85, 92, 119
ethics/morality. *See also specific topics*
   absolute form of, 125
   Fichte's work on, xv–xvii
   formal, 123, 125, 127
   nature of, 11n5
   position of ethics in Fichte's thought, xvii–xix
   theory of
      basic principle of, 68
      historical application of Fichte's, 65
      pure, 63n5, 125
      as science, 3. *See also* science: ethics and
      as a theory of being, 51, 65
   theory of the art of, 61

facts of consciousness, 3, 17
Fichte's lectures on, xvi, xxi, 123n7
faculties, xi. *See also* sight, faculty of
faith, 161, 162
   church and, 161
   doctrine of, 161
   ecclesiastical, xiii, 169
   historical, xiii
   hope and, 85, 141
   moral, xiii, xxiii, 156n5, 159, 161, 168
   organic, 167
   pure, xiii, 169
   reason and, 168
   revelation and, 159, 168–69
falsehoods, 147–48
form. *See also* pure form
   of appearance, 51, 72, 100nn3–4, 101
   objective forms of the world, 65
formal being, 43, 97
formal criterion for will, 113, 115, 116, 119, 123
formal freedom, 22
formal ground, 167
formal life, 17–19, 57, 67
formal morality, 125, 127, 133
formal principles, 19, 27, 38n3
free life, 17
free power, 21–24, 35–36, 49n5
free will. *See* freedom: will and
freedom, xi, 50, 51, 56, 102. *See also* free power; self-determination
   absolute, 17, 41
   appearance and apparent, 54, 66, 110
   causality and, 16–17, 19, 30, 33, 49n4
   community and, 96, 102n6, 117n8
   comprehending the idea of, xxi
   consciousness and, 35–36, 44, 49, 50, 127, 150
   ethics and, xxii, xxviii, 9nn2–3, 42, 44, 51, 53, 57, 89–90, 102n6, 103, 117, 127–28, 150
   Fichte's system of, xvii–xviii
   God and, 89
   ground and, 21–22, 28–30, 39, 41, 42, 50, 89
   and the I, xx, 28–31, 33, 38, 41, 43, 44n3, 50, 54, 67, 73, 80, 89, 94, 96, 101–2, 105n3, 132–33
   idealism and, xvii–xviii
   ideality and, 29–30, 73
   law of, xxviii, 44

of many, 9nn2–3
Plato and, 65
reflection and reflective, 117, 130
will and, 29–31, 35–36, 39, 40, 42, 43, 44n3, 53, 57, 67, 73, 80

God, 70, 74, 87, 89, 147, 160
appearance of, 18, 100n4, 110, 113n1, 119–20
Christianity and, 55n3, 65n1, 66n2, 114
consciousness and, 38, 62, 120, 129n5, 170
creed and, 158, 159
educating humanity, 62–63
ethics and, xxi, xxii, 5, 38, 45, 62, 120, 129nn4–5, 131
freedom and, 89
image of, xxi, xxii, 5, 55n3, 65n1, 66n2, 110, 120, 170
unfree development of the, 129nn4–5
oneness of, 114
pure concept and, xxi, 55n3
revelation and, 162, 170
theory of, 38, 45. See also *Wissenschaftslehre*
will of, 55n3, 66n2, 85, 120, 137, 141–42
gods, 114, 162
ground, 12, 21, 34
absolute, 4, 50
actuality of being a, 12, 13
actualization and, 21, 35, 41
causality and, 11, 37
cognition and, 91, 92n3, 167
and the concept, 15–17, 18n4, 21, 22, 25, 27–30, 33–35, 37, 39–42, 46, 66n2
consciousness and, 3–7, 9–12, 16, 22, 27, 28, 35–37, 39–42
duty and, 91
ethics and, xi, xix, 3, 9, 25n7
formal, 167

freedom and, 21–22, 28–30, 39, 41, 42, 50, 89
and the I, 9, 16, 27–29, 33, 34n1, 35, 37, 39, 41, 91, 93
intuition and, 11–13, 27
life and, xix–xx, 21–22
of the objective concept, 7
ought and, 34n1, 37, 40, 41, 92n3
pure, 25n7
self-determination and, xix–xx, 12, 13n9, 17, 21–22, 29, 35–36
will and, 35, 39–42, 91, 92n3
of the world/of all being, 27, 34, 50, 127
the concept as the, xix–xx, 3–7, 8n13, 9–10, 15, 34n3, 44, 66n2

harmony and harmonization, xiv, xxi–xxii
higher concept, 156, 156–57nn6–7
higher law, 102n7, 150
higher organ, 101, 103, 105n3
higher self, 148–49
hope and faith, 85, 141
Humboldt, Wilhelm von, xi–xii

I, empirical, 31n6, 42n9, 105
I, the, 33–35, 37–38, 54, 72, 131–32. See also life: of the concept; *specific topics*
actuality and, 67, 72n1, 73, 78, 104, 132
actualization and, 28, 29, 37
causality and, 24, 34n4, 73
community of I's, xxi, 96–97, 107–8
consciousness and, xx, 16, 24, 27, 28, 35, 37–40, 46, 54, 55, 79, 80, 83, 93, 94
duty and, 83–84
freedom and, xx, 28–31, 33, 38, 41, 43, 44n3, 50, 54, 67, 73, 80, 89, 94, 96, 101–2, 105n3, 132–33
ground and, 9, 16, 27–29, 33, 34n1, 35, 37, 39, 41, 91, 93

I, the *(continued)*
  intuition and, 28, 28n4, 43, 44, 66, 84
  ought and, 34n4, 35, 37–40, 42n9, 43–45, 59, 73, 78–80, 91–92, 103nn1–2
  pure concept and, 28, 30, 34n4, 41, 92
  as self-sufficient principle, 107
  sensible world and, 84n2, 104
  willing and, 29, 31, 40, 41, 43, 53, 57, 59, 67, 68, 74–75, 77–78, 79n5, 91, 92n3
I *ought*, 34n4, 35, 40, 43–45, 78–80, 103n1. See also *ought*
ideal image, xiv, 35, 68, 131n2, 132n3
idealism
  Fichte's, x, xv–xviii
    ethics and, xiv, xvii–xviii
    freedom and, xvii–xviii
    reason and, xv
  German, vii, viii
ideality (and reality), 34, 87
  freedom and, 29–30, 73
  will, self-determination, and, 27, 29–31, 33, 39–41, 42n9, 57, 68, 73
illusion, theory of, 67–68
image. *See also* God: image of
  absolute, 6, 55, 74n7, 122
  ideal, xiv, 35, 68, 131n2, 132n3
  pure, 4, 6, 66n2, 93
Incarnation, doctrine of the, xx, 54–55
indifference, 53, 73, 74n6, 75, 83, 84n1, 90, 92
indirectness, 71, 72n2
insight, 108–10, 113, 154
  agreement in, 155. *See also* creed
  clear, 146, 147n2
  scientific, xiii, 108
intuition, 11–13, 16, 156n7
  act of will and, 29
  causality and, 11, 16
  consciousness and, 11, 27, 28
  ground and, 11–13, 27
  and the I, 28, 28n4, 43, 44, 66, 84
  intellectual, 29
  objective, 11, 16, 21, 25, 27, 28, 43, 44, 56n7, 104
  sensible, 48, 155n3, 156n7

Jena, University of, x, xvi–xviii, xxviii
Jesus Christ, xxiii, 55n3, 65, 66n2, 158. *See also* John, Gospel of
Jews, 162–63
John, Gospel of, xxiii, 55n3, 65n1, 66n2, 158

Kant, Immanuel, xix, 15–16, 155n3
  on aesthetics, 103n1, 104
  categorical imperative and, xx, 5n6, 37, 38, 45
  The Conflict of the Faculties, ix
  Critique of Practical Reason, 30n5, 38n3, 46n4
  Critique of the Power of Judgment, 103n1, 104, 155n3
  on ethics, xvii–xx, xxviii, 5, 38n3, 38–39, 45–46, 77, 92
  on multiple worlds, 123n7
  on noumenal affection or causation, xxix
  on will and freedom, xi, 30
knowing, system of, 167. *See also Wissenschaftslehre*

Lectures on the Theory of Ethics (Fichte)
  context of, viii–xv
  outline of, xix–xxiii
life, xix, 21–22. *See also specific topics*
  of the concept, 19, 24, 28–30, 33, 43, 50, 51, 54–57, 59, 66n2, 67, 71–75, 77–80, 84, 85, 92–94, 99, 115–17, 119, 125, 132, 143n7
  consciousness and, xx, 24, 27, 49–50, 55, 93
  formal, 17–19, 57, 67
  ground and, xix–xx, 21–22

and the I, 68, 85, 94
moral, 84, 103, 127, 147
unity of, 125
willing and, 114–15
love, xxii, 66, 116–17, 139–42, 144
higher, 141, 142
willing and, 139, 140
lying, 147, 148

miracles, 149–50
moral concept, xiii, xiv, 45, 123n9, 154, 156nn6–7, 168
moral consciousness, xii–xiii, 38–39, 94, 95n3, 122, 154, 156. *See also* consciousness: ethics and
moral formation, xxi, xxi–xxii, 128, 129nn4–5, 160
  stages in the process of, xxi
  theory of, 62
moral foundation (*Grundlage*), 142, 147
moral life, 84, 103, 127, 147
moral phenomenology. *See* appearance
moral sense (*sittliche Sinn*), xxiii, 157, 161, 167
moral vs. immoral appearance, xx–xxi. *See also* appearance
moral will, absolute. *See* absolute will
morality. *See* ethics/morality
motives, xxi, xxii, 40n6, 41–42, 42n9, 57, 59, 91, 92
Muhammad, Prophet, xxi, 114

Napoleon Bonaparte, x, xii, xv, xvii, xxi, 114n3
natural I, 108
natural occurrence, 150
nature. *See* objective world
Naturphilosophie, xvii, xix, 7, 8nn12–13, 34. *See also* Schelling, Friedrich Wilhelm Joseph
nonempirical, 95–96
not-I, 28

objective appearance, 44, 99, 123n8

objective being, 21, 27–28, 30, 34, 71–72, 126
objective concept, 8n12
  vs. pure concept, 6–7
objective consciousness, 28, 33nn1–2, 35, 39, 44, 50
objective form, 44. *See also* intuition: objective; objective consciousness
  vs. pure form, 21
objective forms of the world, 65
objective intuition. *See* intuition: objective
objective knowing, 47
  vs. pure knowing, 65
objective reality and the I, 57
objective representations, 99
objective seeing, 27, 28
objective vs. pure thinking, 47
objective world
  and the concept, 50, 56, 93, 126
  freedom and, 50, 51n7, 56
  ground of, 93. *See also* ground
  and the I, 93, 100–101, 127
  vs. illusory world, 65n1
  nature and, 48
  Plato on, 65
objectivity, 28, 42, 56, 93, 94
ought, 45, 62, 92n3, 104. *See also* I ought
  appearance and, 57
  and the concept, 35, 37–39, 42–45, 56–57, 80, 92n3, 103nn1–2, 116
  consciousness and, 35, 37, 38, 40–41, 57, 79, 80
  duty and, 59, 60
  ethics and, 91, 92n3
  form/formal character of, 92n3
  freedom and, 42, 44, 45n3, 57, 73
  ground and, 34n1, 37, 40, 41, 92n3
  and the I, 34n4, 35, 37–40, 42n9, 43–45, 59, 73, 78–80, 91–92, 103nn1–2
  life and, 73, 79
  representation of the, 40–41

ought (continued)
  science, theology of ethics, and, 9
  will, willing, and, 33, 39–42, 44n2, 45, 57, 59, 60, 91, 92n3, 116

pedagogy, x, xiii–xiv, xxviii, 62. *See also* education
Pestalozzi, J. H., x
philanthropy, universal, xiv–xv, xxii, 139. *See also* love
philosophical science, 3
philosophy, xiii. *See also* church; *specific topics*
  academic, ix. *See also* university education
  creed and, xiii, xxiii, 167–69
  as pure thinking, 16
  reason and, 168–70
  revelation and, 167, 169
  science and, xi, xii, xix, 3, 167–68
Plato, 56n7, 65
power. *See also* authority
  free, 21–24, 35–36, 49n5
practical reason. *See also* reason
  Critique of Practical Reason (Kant), 30n5, 38n3, 46n4
  primacy of, xv
precondition, universal (*Vorbegriff*), 155
principium essendi (principle of being), 101
principle, absolute, 79, 94, 110
principles, 19
  formal, 19, 27, 38n3
pure concept, 7, 108, 115–16. *See also* absolute concept; pure form
  absolute content of, 18
  appearance of, xxi
  consciousness and, 6–7, 96n4
  empirical I and, 31n6
  ethics and, xx, xxi, 55n3, 92
  God and, xxi, 55n3
  ground of the world and, xix
  and the I, 28, 30, 34n4, 41, 92

  life and, 18
  self-determination and, xix, xx, 23
  will and, xx, 31
pure faith, xiii
pure form, 21n1, 44, 80, 116
pure ground, 25n7
pure image, 4, 6, 66n2, 93
pure morality, 63n5
pure seeing, 28

reason, 15, 90, 108. *See also* practical reason
  definitions and meanings of, 55, 90
  duty and, 153n1
  ethics and, xiv, xvii, 9
  faith and, 168
  idealism and, xviii
  philosophy and, 168–70
  as practical, xviii, xix, 9, 15–16, 55–56
  understanding and, 56, 90
reciprocity/reciprocal interaction (*Wechselwirkung*), 111, 154
  continued/continual, 154
  moral, 155, 160
reflection and reflective freedom, 117, 130. *See also* self-consciousness
reflexivity, 96
religion. *See* Christianity; church; creed; spirit
religious symbolism, 155n3. *See also* creed
representation, obscure, 134–35
representational concept, xxii, 4
representationality, 93, 96, 99, 100, 101n5
revelation, xvii, 161–62
  church and, xxii–xxiii, 157–59, 161, 163, 165
  creed and, xxii–xxiii, 157–59, 167
  doctrine of, 157–59, 161
  ethics and, 159, 167, 168
  faith and, 159, 168–69
  God and, 162, 170

history of, 163–65
nature of, xxii–xxiii
philosophy and, 167, 169

Salzmann, Christian Gotthilf, x
Schelling, Friedrich Wilhelm Joseph, ix, xvii, 7n11, 48
Schleiermacher, Friedrich, ix, xi
science, xiv, 3, 4, 6
    creed and, xii, 161
    ethics and, xii, xiv, xix, 5, 60, 61
    philosophy and, xi, xii, xix, 3, 167–68
Science of Knowing, The. See *Wissenschaftslehre*: Fichte's lectures on
scientific insight, xiii, 108
seeing. *See also* sight
    objective, 27, 28
self, higher, 148–49
self-appearance, 132
self-consciousness, 31, 79, 86, 93–94, 125, 129
self-cultivation, xiv–xv, xxii
self-denial, 131
self-determination, 12, 13n9, 16–17, 19, 21–23, 27, 38. *See also under* ideality
    absolute, xx, 12, 16–17, 22, 29, 31, 35, 39
    ethics and, xx, xxii
    God and, xxi
    ground and, xix–xx, 12, 13n9, 17, 21–22, 29, 35–36
    ideal concept and, 31, 33
    life and, xix
    pure concept and, xix, xx, 23
    will, willing, and, xx, 29–31, 35–36, 39, 40, 80, 91, 92n3
self-seeing, all seeing as, 96
self-sufficient principle, 107
selflessness (*Selbstlosigkeit*), 31–33
sensible, the, 169
sensible world, 89, 150
    Christianity and, 65n1, 66n2

collective consciousness of, 154. *See also* collective consciousness
and the concept, 65n1, 66n2, 84n2
God and, 55n3
and the I, 84n2, 104
natural consciousness and, 156
ratiocination about, 169
will and, 55n3, 84n2
sight. *See also* seeing
    faculty of, 94–96
    vs. feeling, 167–68
spirit (*geist*), 6–8, 49, 105, 107, 109, 111, 113, 120, 121n4, 126, 127, 143
spirit world/spiritual world, 47–49
spiritual (*geistigen*) life, 144
superempirical (*überempirische*), 97, 99, 108
supersensible, the, xiii, xx, 93, 100n4, 156, 159, 162, 169
superstition, 90, 170–71
System of Ethics according to the Principles of the Wissenschaftslehre, The (Fichte), xvi, xvii, xix, 153

thinking, types of, 47
time. *See* eternity
transcendental philosophy, xvi
true being, 51, 53, 69, 83

understanding, 56
unification (*Vereinigung*), 154
unity
    absolute, 29, 38, 116n7
    eternal, 119
    of life, 125
university education, ix–xi
University of Berlin, viii, ix, xii, xv, xvi, xxviii
University of Jena, x, xvi–xviii, xxviii

visibility, 95–97, 99, 100, 100n4, 105
    of being, 51
    of the concept, 67, 68, 91
vision. *See* seeing; sight

will. *See also under* ideality
   absolute, 80, 83, 84n1, 85–87, 91, 92n3, 125, 133, 142, 145
   formal criterion for, 113, 115, 116, 119, 123
   of God, 55n3, 66n2, 85, 120, 137, 141–42
   ground and, 35, 39–42, 91, 92n3
   meaning and nature of, xx
   pure concept and, xx, 31
   sensible world and, 55n3, 84n2
willing (*Wollen*), 33n2, 80. *See also under* ideality; will
   causality and, 30n5
   and the concept, 31, 35, 74–75, 77–78, 79n5, 114–15, 121–22, 126, 127n3
   consciousness and, 33nn1–2, 35–36, 40–42, 80, 113–15, 128, 129n5
   duty and, xxi, 59, 60, 80, 91, 116, 121–23, 134, 150
   ethics and, 31n6, 53, 77, 116, 127n3, 133, 134, 140, 149
   freedom and, 29–31, 35–36, 39, 40, 42, 43, 44n3, 53, 57, 67, 73, 80
   and the I, 29, 31, 40, 41, 43, 53, 57, 59, 67, 68, 74–75, 77–78, 79n5, 91, 92n3
   knowledge and, 149
   life and, 114–15
   love and, 139, 140
   motive of, 42n9, 57. *See also* motives
   ought and, 33, 39–42, 44n2, 45, 57, 59, 60, 91, 92n3, 116
   self-determination and, xx, 29–31, 35–36, 39, 40, 80, 91, 92n3
Wissenschaftslehre, xii, xvi, 3, 6, 10, 16, 38, 45–46, 132, 167
   Fichte's lectures on, vii, xv, xvi, xviii–xix
   main points of, 18
   philosophy and, 38, 167
world, 43. *See also* ground: of the world/of all being; objective world; sensible world